A Journey in Southeastern Mexico

Henry Howard Harper

Alpha Editions

This edition published in 2022

ISBN: 9789356571143

Design and Setting By

Alpha Editions
www.alphaedis.com

Email - info@alphaedis.com

As per information held with us this book is in Public Domain.
This book is a reproduction of an important historical work.
Alpha Editions uses the best technology to reproduce historical work
in the same manner it was first published to preserve its original nature.
Any marks or number seen are left intentionally to preserve.

Table of Contents

AUTHOR'S PREFACE — 1 —

INTRODUCTORY NOTE — 4 —

A JOURNEY IN SOUTHEASTERN MEXICO — 6 —

FOOTNOTES: — 51 —

AUTHOR'S PREFACE

The volume here presented to the reader does not profess to be a history or description of Mexico as a whole, nor does it claim to be typical of all sections of the country. It deals simply with an out-of-the-way and little-known region, accompanied by a history of personal experiences, with comment upon conditions almost or quite unknown to the ordinary traveler.

Many books upon Mexico have been written—a few by competent and others by incompetent hands—in which the writers sometimes charge each other with misstatements and inaccuracies, doubtless oftentimes with reason. However that may be, I have yet to discover among them a narrative, pure and simple, of travel, experiences and observations in the more obscure parts of that country, divested of long and tedious topographical descriptions. Narrations which might be of interest, once begun, are soon lost in discussion of religious, political, and economic problems, or in singing the praises of "the redoubtable Cortez," or the indefatigable somebody else who is remembered chiefly for the number of people he caused to be killed; or in describing the beauty of some great valley or hill which the reader perhaps never saw and never will see.

I have always felt that a book should never be printed unless it is designed to serve some worthy purpose, and that as soon as the author has written enough to convey his message clearly he should stop. There are many books in which the essential points could be encompassed within half the number of pages allotted to their contents. A good twenty-minute sermon is better than a fairly good two-hour sermon; hence I believe in short sermons,—and short books.

With this conviction, before placing this manuscript in the hands of the printer I sought to ascertain what possible good might be accomplished by its issue in printed form. My first thought was to consult some authority, upon the frankness and trustworthiness of whose opinion I could rely with certainty. I therefore placed the manuscript in the hands of my friend Mr. Charles E. Hurd, whose excellent scholarship and sound literary judgment, coupled with a lifelong experience as an editor and critical reviewer, qualify him as an authority second to none in this country. He has done me the honor voluntarily to prepare a few introductory lines which are printed herein.

In view of the probability that very few, if any, among the restricted circle who read this book will ever traverse the territory described, I am forced to conclude that for the present it can serve no better purpose than that of affording such entertainment as may be derived from the mere reading of the narrative. If, however, it should by chance fall into the hands of any individual who contemplates traveling, or investing money, in this district, it might prove to be of a value equal to the entire cost of the issue. Moreover, it may serve a useful purpose in enlightening and entertaining those who are content to leave to others the pleasures of travel as well as the profits derived from investments in the rural agricultural districts of Mexico.

Possibly a hundred years hence the experiences, observations, and modes of travel herein noted will be so far outgrown as to make them seem curious to the traveler who may cover the same territory, but I predict that even a thousand years from now the conditions there will not undergo so radical a change that the traveler may not encounter the same identical customs and the same aggravating pests and discomforts that are so prevalent today. Doubtless others have traversed this territory with similar motives, and have made practically the same mental observations, but I do not find that anyone has taken the pains to record them either as a note of warning to others, or as a means of replenishing a depleted exchequer.

In issuing this book I feel somewhat as I imagine Horace did when he wrote his ode to Pyrrha,—which was perhaps not intended for the eye of Pyrrha at all, but was designed merely as a warning to others against her false charms, or against the wiles of any of her sex. He declared he had paid the price of his folly and inexperience, and had hung up his dripping clothes in the temple as a danger-signal for others—

Ah! wretched those who love, yet ne'er did tryThe smiling treachery of thine eye;But I'm secure, my danger's o'er,My table shows the clothesI vow'dWhen midst the storm, to please the god,I have hung up, and now am safe on shore.

So am I. Horace, being a confirmed bachelor, probably took his theme from some early love affair which would serve as a key-note that would strike at the heart and experience of almost every reader. The apparent ease with which one can make money and enjoy trips in Mexico is scarcely less deceptive than were the bewitching smiles of Horace's Pyrrha. Indeed the fortune-seeker there can see chimerical Pyrrhas everywhere.

Although it has been said that truth is stranger than fiction, it is observable that most of the great writers have won their fame in fiction, possibly because they could not find truths enough to fill a volume. In setting down the narrative of a journey through Mexico, however, there is no occasion to distort facts in order to make them appear strange, and often incredible, to the reader. We are so surfeited with books of fiction that I sometimes feel it is a wholesome diversion to pick up a book containing a few facts, even though they be stated in plain homespun language. It is fair to assume that in writing a book the author's chief purpose is to convey a message of some sort in language that is understandable. In the following pages I have therefore not attempted any flourishes with the English language, but have simply recorded the facts and impressions in a discursive conversational style, just as I should relate them verbally, or write them in correspondence to some friend.

H. H. H.

Boston, Mass.,
October, 1909.

INTRODUCTORY NOTE

BY CHARLES E. HURD

The present volume in which Mr. Harper tells the story of his personal experiences and observations in a section of Mexico which is now being cleverly exploited in the advertising columns of the newspapers as the great agricultural and fruit-growing region of the North American continent, has a peculiar value, and one that gives it a place apart from the ordinary records of travel. The journey described was no pleasure trip. The three who took part in it were young, ambitious, and full of energy. Each had a fair amount of capital to invest, and each, inspired by the accounts of visitors and the advertisements of land speculators setting forth the wonderful opportunities for easy money making in agricultural ventures along the eastern coast of Mexico, believed that here was a chance to double it. There was no sentiment in the matter; it was from first to last purely a business venture. The scenery might be enchanting, the climate perfect, and the people possessed of all the social requirements, but while these conditions would be gratefully accepted, they were regarded by the party as entirely secondary—they were after money. The recorded impressions are therefore the result of deliberate and thoughtful investigation,—not of the superficial sort such as one would acquire on a pleasure-seeking trip. They differ essentially from the unpractical views of the writer who is sent into Mexico to prepare a glowing account of the country's resources from a casual and personally disinterested view of conditions.

The story of the trip by land and water from Tampico to Tuxpam is photographic in its realism. In no book on Mexico has the character of the peon been as accurately drawn as in this volume. Most writers have been content to sketch in the head and bust of the native Mexican, but here we have him painted by the deft hand of the author at full length, with all his trickery, his laziness and his drunkenness upon him. One cannot help wondering why he was ever created or what he was put here for. In this matter of character-drawing Mr. Harper's book is unique.

The results of the investigations in this section of the country to which the party had been lured are graphically set forth by Mr. Harper in a half-serious, half-humorous manner which gives the narrative a peculiar interest. He perhaps feels that he has been "stung," but yet he feels that he can stand it, and enters no complaint. Besides, the experience is worth something.

Of course the volume does not cover all Mexico, but its descriptions are fairly typical of the larger portion of the country, particularly as regards the people, their habits, morals and methods of living. Aside from its interest as a narrative the book has an important mission. It should be in the hands of every prospective investor in Mexican property, especially those whose ears are open to the fascinating promises and seductive tales of the companies formed for agricultural development. A single reading will make nine out of ten such restrap their pocketbooks. The reader will be well repaid for the time spent in a perusal of the volume, and it is to be regretted that the author has determined to print it only for private and restricted distribution.

Boston, October 25, 1909.

A JOURNEY IN SOUTHEASTERN MEXICO

There are few civilized countries where the American pleasure-seeking traveler is so seldom seen as in the rural districts of southeastern Mexico, along the coast between Tampico and Vera Cruz. The explanation for this is doubtless to be found in the fact that there is perhaps no other civilized country where the stranger is subjected to so many personal discomforts and vexations resulting from incommodious facilities for travel, and from the multiplicity of pests that beset his path.

The writers of books on Mexican travel usually keep pretty close to the beaten paths of travel, and discreetly avoid the by-ways in those portions far removed from any railroad or highway. They acquire their observations and impressions chiefly from the window of the comfortable passenger-coach or from the veranda of some hotel where three good meals are served daily, or from government reports and hearsay,—which are often unreliable. It is only the more daring fortune-hunters that brave the dangers and discomforts of the remote regions, and from these we are rarely favored with a line, either because they have no aptitude for writing, or, as is more likely, because, wishing to forget their experiences as speedily as possible, they make no permanent record of them. Tourists visiting Mexico City, Monterey, Tampico and other large cities are about as well qualified to discourse upon the conditions prevailing in the agricultural sections of the unfrequented country districts as a foreigner visiting Wall Street would be to write about the conditions in the backwoods of northern Maine. I can readily understand the tendency of writers to praise the beauty of Mexican scenery and to expatiate upon the wonderful possibilities in all agricultural pursuits. In passing rapidly from one section to another without seeing the multifarious difficulties encountered from seedtime to harvest, they get highly exaggerated ideas from first impressions, which in Mexico are nearly always misleading. The first time I beheld this country, clothed in the beauty of its tropical verdure, I wondered that everybody didn't go there to live, and now I marvel that anybody should live there, except possibly for a few months in winter. If one would obtain reliable intelligence about Mexico and its advantages—or rather its disadvantages—for profitable agriculture, let him get the honest opinion of some one who has tried the experiment on the spot, of investing either his money or his time, or both, with a view to profit.

In March, 1896, in company with two friends and an interpreter, I went to Mexico, having been lured there by numerous exaggerated reports of the possibilities in the vanilla, coffee and rubber industries. None of us had any intention of remaining there for more than a few months,—long enough to secure plantations, put them in charge of competent superintendents, and outline the work to be pursued. We shared the popular fallacy that if the natives, with their crude and antiquated methods could produce even a small quantity of vanilla, coffee or rubber, we could, by employing more progressive and up-to-date methods, cause these staple products to be yielded in abundant quantities and at so slight a cost as to make them highly profitable. We had heard that the reason why American investors had failed to make money there was because they had invested their funds injudiciously, through intermediaries, and had no personal knowledge of the actual state of affairs at the seat of investment. We were therefore determined to investigate matters thoroughly by braving the dangers and discomforts of pestilence and insects and looking the ground over in person. We had no idea of forming any company or copartnership, but each was to make his own observations and draw his own conclusions quite independent of the others. We agreed, however, to remain together and to assist one another as much as possible by comparing notes and impressions. There was a tacit understanding that all ordinary expenses of travel should be shared equally from one common fund, to which each should contribute his share, but that each one should individually control his own investment, if such were made. Each member of the party had endeavored to post himself as best he could regarding the necessities of the trip. We consulted such accounts of travel in Mexico as were available (nothing, however, was found relating to the locality that we were to visit), conversed with a couple of travelers who had visited the western and central parts, and corresponded with various persons in that country; but when we came together to compare notes of our requirements for the journey no two seemed to agree in any particular. Our objective point was Tuxpam, which is on the eastern coast almost midway between Tampico and Vera Cruz, and a hundred miles from any railroad center. As it was our intention to barter direct with the natives instead of through any land syndicate, we thought best to provide ourselves with an ample supply of the native currency. Out of the thousand and one calculations and estimates that we all made, this latter was about the only one that proved to be anywhere near correct. In changing our money into Mexican currency we were of course eager to secure the highest premium, and upon learning that American gold was much in demand at Tampico (the point where we were to leave the railroad) we shipped a quantity of gold coin by express to that place.

Our journey to Tampico was by rail via Laredo and Monterey, and was without special incident; the reader need not therefore be detained by a recital of what we thought or saw along this much traveled highway. This route—especially as far as Monterey—is traversed by many Americans, and American industry is seen all along the line, notably at Monterey.

Upon arriving at Tampico we were told by the money-changers there that they had no use for American gold coin. They said that the only way in which they could use our money was in the form of exchange on some eastern city, which could be used by their merchants in making remittances for merchandise; so we were obliged to ship it all back to an eastern bank, and sold our checks against a portion of it at a premium of eighty cents on the dollar.

We stalked around town with our pockets bulging out with Mexican national bank notes, and felt quite opulent. Our wealth had suddenly increased to almost double, and it didn't seem as if we ever could spend it, dealing it out after the manner of the natives, three, six, nine and twelve cents at a time. We acquired the habit of figuring every time we spent a dollar that we really had expended only fifty cents. Our fears that we should have difficulty in spending very much money must have shone out through our countenances, for the natives seemed to read them like an open book; and for every article and service they charged us double price and over. We soon found we were spending real dollars, and before returning home we learned to figure the premium the other way.

The moment we began to transact business with these people we became aware that we were in the land of *mañana* (tomorrow). The natives make it a practice never to do anything today that can be put off until tomorrow. Nothing can be done *today*,—it is always "*mañana*," which, theoretically, means tomorrow, but in common practice its meaning is vague,—possibly a day, a week, or a month. Time is reckoned as of no consequence whatever, and celerity is a virtue wholly unknown.

Our business and sightseeing concluded, we made inquiry as to the way to get to Tuxpam, a small coast town in the State of Vera Cruz, about a hundred miles further south. We inquired of a number of persons and learned of nearly as many undesirable or impossible ways of getting there. There were coastwise steamers from Tuxpam up to Tampico, but none down the coast from Tampico to Tuxpam. After spending a whole day in fruitless endeavor to find a means of transportation we were returning to the hotel late in the afternoon, when a native came running up behind us and asked if we were the Americans who wanted to go to Tuxpam. He said that he had a good sailboat and was to sail for Tuxpam *mañana* via the *laguna*,—a chain of lakes extending along near the coast from Tampico to Tuxpam, connected by channels ranging in length from a hundred yards to several miles, which in places are very shallow, or totally dry, most of the time. We went back with him to his boat, which we found to be a sturdy-looking craft about thirty feet long, with perhaps a five-foot beam. It was constructed of two large cedar logs hewn out and mortised together. The boatman said he had good accommodations aboard and would guarantee to land us at Tuxpam in seven days. He wanted two hundred dollars (Mexican money, of course) to take our party of four. This was more than the whole outfit was worth, with his wages for three weeks thrown in. We went aboard, and were looking over the boat, rather to gratify our curiosity than with any intention of accepting his monstrous offer, when one of the party discovered a Mexican lying in the bottom of the boat with a shawl loosely thrown over him. Our interpreter inquired if anyone was sick aboard, and was told by the owner that the man was a friend of his who was ill with the smallpox, and that he was taking him to his family in Tuxpam. We stampeded in great confusion and on our way to the hotel procured a supply of sulphur, carbolic acid, chlorine, and all the disinfectants we could think of. Hurrying to one of our rooms in the hotel, we barred the door and discussed what we should do to ward off the terrible disease. Some one suggested that perhaps the boatman was only joking, and that after all the man didn't have smallpox. It didn't seem plausible that he would ask us to embark for a seven days' voyage in company with a victim of an infectious disease. But who would venture back to ascertain the facts? Of course this task fell upon the interpreter, as he was the only one who could speak the language. While he was gone we began preparing for the worst, and after taking account of our stock of disinfectants the question was which to use and how to apply it. Each one recommended a different formula. One of the party found some sort of a tin vessel, and putting half a pound of sulphur into it, set it afire and put it under the bed. We then took alternate sniffs of the several disinfectants, and debated as to whether we should return home at once, or await developments. Meanwhile the room had become filled almost to suffocation with the sulphur fumes, the burning sulphur had melted the solder off the tin vessel, and running out had set the floor on fire. About this time there was a vigorous rap at the door and some one asked a question in Spanish; but none of us could either ask or answer questions in that language, so there was no chance for an argument and we all kept quiet, except for the scuffling around in the endeavor to extinguish the fire. The water-pitcher being empty, as usual, some one seized my new overcoat and threw it over the flames. At this juncture our interpreter returned and informed us that it was no joke about the sick man, and that the police authorities had just discovered him and ordered him to the hospital. He found that the boatman had already had smallpox and was not afraid of it; he was quite surprised at our sudden alarm. As the interpreter came in, the man who had knocked reappeared, and said that having smelled the sulphur fumes he thought someone was committing suicide. When we told him what had happened he laughed hysterically, but unfortunately we were unable to share the funny side of the joke with him.

That evening when we went down to supper everybody seemed to regard us with an air of curious suspicion, and we imagined that we were tagged all over with visible smallpox bacteria.

We afterwards learned that the natives pay little more heed to smallpox than we do to measles; and especially in the outlying country districts, they appear to feel toward it much as we do toward measles and whooping-cough,—that the sooner they have it and are over with it (or rather, it is over with them), the better. One of the party vowed that he wouldn't go to his room to sleep alone that night, because he knew he should have the smallpox before morning. After supper we borrowed a small earthenware vessel and returning to our "council chamber" we started another smudge with a combination of sulphur and other fumigating drugs. Someone expressed regret that he had ever left home on such a fool's errand. During the night it had been noised about that there was a party of "Americanos ricos" (rich Americans) who wanted to go to Tuxpam, and next morning there were a number of natives waiting to offer us various modes of conveyance, all alike expensive and tedious. We finally decided to go via the *laguna* in a small boat, and finding that one of the men was to start that afternoon we went down with him to see his boat, which proved to be of about the same construction and dimensions as the one we had looked at the previous afternoon. He said that he had scarcely any cargo and would take us through in a hurry; that he would take three men along and if the wind was unfavorable they would use the paddles in poling the boat. His asking price for our passage, including provisions, was $150, but when he saw that we wouldn't pay that much he dropped immediately to $75; so we engaged passage with him, on his promising to land us in Tuxpam in six days. He said there was plenty of water in the channels connecting the lakes, except at one place where there would be a very short carry, and that he had arranged for a man and team to draw the boat over. We ordered our baggage sent to the boat and not liking his bill of fare we set out to provide ourselves with our own provisions for the trip.

When we arrived at the boat we found our baggage stored away, with a variety of merchandise, including a hundred bags of flour, piled on top of it. There was not a foot of vacant space in the bottom of the boat, and we were expected to ride, eat and sleep for six days and nights on top of the cargo. The boatman had cunningly stored our effects underneath the merchandise hoping that we would not back out when we saw the cargo he was to take. However, we had become thoroughly disgusted with the place and conditions (the hotel man having arbitrarily charged us $25 for the hole we burned in his cheap pine floor), and were glad to get out of town by any route and at any cost. We all clambered aboard and were off at about three p.m. As we sat perched up on top of that load of luggage and merchandise when the boat pulled out of the harbor we must have looked more like pelicans sitting on a huge floating log than like "Americanos ricos" in search of rubber, vanilla and coffee lands. We didn't find as much rubber in the whole Republic of Mexico as there appeared to be in the necks of those idlers who had gathered on the shore to see us off.

The propelling equipment of our boat consisted of a small sail, to be used in case of favorable breezes—which we never experienced—and two long-handled cedar paddles. The blades of these were about ten inches wide and two and a half feet long, while the handles were about twelve feet long. The natives are very skillful in handling these paddles. They usually work in pairs,—one on each side of the boat. One starts at the bow by pressing the point of the paddle against the bottom and walks along the edge of the boat to the stern, pushing as he walks. By the time he reaches the stern his companion continues the motion of the boat by the same act, beginning at the bow on the opposite side. By the time the first man has walked back to the bow the second has reached the stern, and so on. The boats are usually run in the shallow water along near the shore of the large bodies of water in the chain of lakes, so that the paddles will reach the bottom. The boatman had three men besides himself in order to have two shifts, and promised that the boat should run both night and day. This plan worked beautifully in theory, but how well it worked out in practice will be seen later on. We glided along swimmingly until we reached the first channel a short distance from Tampico, and here we were held up for two hours getting over a shoal. That seemed a long wait, but before we reached our destination we learned to measure our delays not by hours but by days. After getting over the first obstruction we dragged along the channel for an hour or so and then came to a full stop. We were told that there was another shallow place just ahead and that we must wait awhile for the tide to float us over. We prepared our supper, which consisted of ham, canned baked beans, bread, crackers, and such delicacies as we had obtained at the stores in Tampico. The supper prepared by the natives consisted of strips of dried beef cut into small squares and boiled with rice and black beans. At first we were inclined to scorn such fare as they had intended for us, but before we reached Tuxpam there were times when it seemed like a Presidential banquet. After supper three of the boatmen went ahead, ostensibly to see how much water there was in the channel, while the fourth remained with the boat. After starting a mosquito smudge and discussing the situation for a couple of hours, we decided to "turn in" for the night. The interpreter asked the remaining Mexican where the bedding was. His only response was a sort of bewildered grin. He didn't seem to understand what bedding was, and said they never carried it. We were expected to "roost" on top of the cargo without even so much as a spread over us,—which we did. It was an eventful night,—one of the many of the kind that were to follow. After the fire died out we fought mosquitoes—the hugest I had ever seen—until about three o'clock in the morning, when I fell asleep from sheer exhaustion. There being no frost in this section to kill these venomous insects, they appear to grow and multiply from year to year until finally they die of old age. A description of their size and numbers would test the most elastic human credulity. Webster must have had in mind this variety when he described the mosquito as having "a proboscis containing, within the sheathlike labium, six fine sharp needlelike organs with which they puncture the skin of man and animals to suck the blood."

I had been asleep but a short time when the party returned from the inspection of the "water" ahead, and if the fire-water they had aboard had been properly distributed it would almost have floated us over any shoal in the channel. They brought with them two more natives who were to help carry the cargo over the shallow place, but all five of them were in the same drunken condition. In less than ten minutes they all were sound asleep on the grass beside the channel. We were in hopes that such a tempting bait might distract some of the mosquitoes from ourselves, but no such luck. The mosquitoes had no terrors for them and they slept on as peacefully as the grass on which they lay. All hands were up at sunrise and we supposed of course we were to be taken over the shoal; but in this we were disappointed, for this proved to be some saint's day, observed by all good Mexicans as a day of rest and feasting. We endeavored to get them to take us back to town, but no one would be guilty of such sacrilege as working on a feast-day. When asked when we could proceed on the journey they said "*Mañana.*" After breakfast our party strolled off into the pasture along the channel and when we returned to the boat a few minutes later the Mexicans shouted in a chorus "*Garrapatas! mucho malo!*" at the same time pointing to our clothes, which were literally covered with small wood-ticks, about half the size of an ordinary pinhead.

Garra—pronounced gar-r-r-ra—means to hook or grab hold of, and *patas* means "feet," so I take it that this pestilential insect is so named because it grabs hold and holds tight with its feet. If this interpretation be correct, it is well named, because the manner in which it lays hold with its feet justifies its name, not to mention the tenacity with which it hangs on with its head. It is very difficult to remove one from the skin before it gets "set," and after fastening itself securely the operation of removing it is both irritating and painful. If it should ever need renaming some word should be found that signifies "grab hold and hang on with both head and feet."

They cling to the grass and leaves of bushes in small clusters after the manner of a swarm of bees, and the instant anything touches one of these clusters they let go all hold and drop off onto the object, and proceed at once to scatter in every direction; taking care, however, not to fall a second time. We had noticed a few bites, but paid no special attention to them, as we were becoming accustomed to being "bitten." Many of them had now reached the skin, however, and they claimed our particular attention for the remainder of the day. We inquired how best to get rid of them and were told that our clothes would have to be discarded. The loss of the clothes and the wood-ticks adhering to them was not a matter of such immediate consequence as those which had already found their way through the seams and openings and reached the skin. We were told that to bathe in kerosene or turpentine would remove them if done before they got firmly set, and that if they were not removed we would be inoculated with malaria and thrown into a violent fever, for being unacclimated, their bite would be poisonous to our systems. Of course there was not a drop of kerosene or turpentine aboard, so the direst consequences were inevitable. Our trip was fast becoming interesting, and with the cheering prospects of malarial fever and smallpox ahead, we began to wonder what was next! All interest in the progress of the journey was now entirely subverted, and, with the mosquitoes and *garrapatas* to play the accompaniment to other bodily woes and discomforts, sufficient entertainment was in store for the coming night.

After digging out our trunks and changing our clothes we thoughtlessly laid our cast-off garments on top of the cargo, with the result that in a short time the whole boat was infested with the little pests. Our one comforting hope was that they might torture the Mexicans, but this proved to be a delusive consolation, for we found that the natives were accustomed to their bites and paid but little attention to them. I refrain from detailing the events and miseries of the night following, because I wish to forget them. Not least among our annoyances was the evident relish with which the Mexicans regarded our discomforts during daylight, and the blissful serenity with which they slept through it all at night. As they lay there calmly asleep while we kept a weary vigil with the mosquitoes and ticks, I was strongly tempted to push one of them off into the water just to disturb his aggravating rest. They laughed uproariously at our actions and imprecations over the wood-ticks, but the next laugh was to be at their expense, as will be seen further along.

Next morning at sunrise (from sunrise to sunset is regarded by the Mexicans as the duration of a day's work) they began unloading the cargo and carrying it half a mile over the shoal. The strength and endurance of the men were remarkable, considering their meagre fare. Each man would carry from two to three hundred pounds on the back of his neck and shoulders the entire distance of half a mile without stopping to rest. By two o'clock in the afternoon the cargo was transferred and the boat dragged over the shoal. In this latter undertaking we all lent a hand. If any of our friends at home could have witnessed this scene in which we took an active part, with our trousers rolled up, wading in mud and water nearly up to our knees, they might well have wondered what Eldorado we were headed for.

By the time the boatmen got the cargo reloaded it was time for supper, and they were too tired to continue the voyage that night.

We slept intermittently during the night, and fought mosquitoes between dozes. We started next morning about five o'clock. This was the beginning of the fourth day out and we had covered less than six miles. One of the men told us that on the last trip they took ten days in making the same distance. It began to look as though we would have to go on half rations in order to make our food supply last through the journey. We moved along the channel without interruption during the day, and late in the afternoon reached the point where the channel opened into a large lake several miles long. We camped that night by the lakeside,—the Mexicans having apparently forgotten their promise to pursue the journey at night. They slept on the bare ground, while we remained in the boat. A brisk breeze blew from the lake, so we had no mosquitoes to disturb the first peaceful night's sleep we had enjoyed since the smallpox scare.

During the night we made the acquaintance of another native pest, known as the "army-ant," a huge black variety measuring upwards of half an inch in length, the bite of which produces much the same sensation as the sting of a hornet or scorpion, though the pain is of shorter duration. The shock produced by the bite, even of a single one, is sudden and violent, and there is nothing that will cause a Mexican to disrobe with such involuntary promptness as the attack of one of these pestiferous insects. They move through the country at certain seasons in great bodies, covering the ground for a space of from fifty feet to a hundred yards wide, and perhaps double the length. If a house happens to stand in their way they will rid it completely of rats, mice, roaches, scorpions, and even the occupants. They invade every crevice from cellar to garret, and every insect, reptile and animal is compelled either to retreat or be destroyed. Nothing will cause a household to vacate a dwelling more suddenly at any time of the night or day, than the approach of the dreaded army-ant.

The boatmen were all asleep on the bank of the lake, while we, remaining aboard the boat, had finished our after-supper smoke and were preparing to retire. Suddenly our attention was attracted by a shout from the four Mexicans almost simultaneously, which echoing through the woods on the night air, produced the weirdest sound I had ever heard. It was a cry of sudden alarm and extreme pain. In an instant the four natives were on their feet, and their shirts were removed with almost the suddenness of a flash of lightning. They all headed for the boat and plunged headlong into the water. The army-ant being unknown to us, and not knowing the cause of their sudden alarm, we were uncertain whether they had all gone crazy or were fleeing from some wild beast. They scrambled aboard the boat, and one of the regrets of my life was that I couldn't understand Spanish well enough to appreciate the full force of their ejaculations. All four of them jabbered in unison—rubbing first one part of the body and then another—for fully ten minutes, and judging from their maledictions and gestures, I doubt if any of them had a good word to say about the ants. It was now our turn to laugh. In half an hour or so they ventured back to the land and recovered their clothes, the army of ants having passed on. They were up most of the night nursing their bites, and once our interpreter called out and asked them if ants were as bad as *garrapatas*. One of the men was so severely poisoned by the numerous bites that he was obliged to return home the next day.

At about eight o'clock next morning we arrived at a little village, or settlement, and after wandering around for half an hour our party returned to the boat, but the boatmen were nowhere to be seen. We waited there until nearly noon, and then started out in search of them. They were presently found in the store, all drunk and asleep in a back room. We aroused them, but they were in no condition to proceed, and had no intention of doing so. We remained there just twenty-eight hours, and when we again started on our journey it was with only three boatmen, none of them sober enough to work. The wind blew a steady gale in our faces all the afternoon, and we had traveled only about four miles by nightfall. We had now been out more than six days and had not covered one quarter of the distance to Tuxpam. At this rate it would take us nearly a month to reach there.

About three o'clock next day we went ashore at a little settlement, and upon learning that there was to be a *baile* (a dance) that night, the boatmen decided to stay until morning. It was an impoverished looking settlement of perhaps forty huts, mostly of bamboo with thatched roofs of grass. A hut generally had but one room, where the whole family cooked, ate and slept on the dirt floor. This room had an aperture for ingress and egress, the light and ventilation being admitted through the cracks. We did not see a bed in the entire village, and in passing some of the huts that night we observed that the entire family slept on the hard dirt floor in the center of the room with no covering. In one hovel, measuring about 12 x 14 feet, we counted eleven people asleep on the floor,—three grown persons and eight children, while the family pig and the dog reposed peacefully in one corner. All were dressed in the same clothes they wore in the daytime, including the dog and pig. The garments of the men usually consist of a pair of knee-drawers,—generally of a white cotton fabric,—a white shirt-waist, leather sandals fastened on their feet with strings of rawhide, and a sombrero, the latter usually being more expensive than all the rest of the wearing apparel. The natives here are generally very cleanly, and change and wash their garments frequently. The women spend most of their time at this work, and when we landed we counted fourteen women washing clothes at the edge of the lake.

The dance began about nine o'clock and most of the participants, both men and women, were neatly attired in white garments. The men were very jealous of their girls, though for what reason it was hard to understand. Many writers rhapsodise over the beauty and loveliness of the Mexican women, but I couldn't see it. There are rare exceptions, however. The dance-hall consisted of a smooth dirt floor with no covering overhead, and the orchestra—a violin and some sort of a wind-instrument—was mounted on a large box in the center. A row of benches extended around the outside of the "dancing-ground." The men all carried their machetes (large cutlasses, the blades of which range from eighteen to thirty-six inches in length) in sheaths at their side, and two or three of the more gaily dressed wore colored sashes around their waists. All wore their sombreros. The dance had not progressed for more than an hour when one of the villagers discovered that his lady was engaging too much of the attention of one of our boatmen, and this resulted in a quarrel. Both men drew their machetes and went at one another in gladiator fashion. It looked as if both would be carved to pieces, but after slashing at each other for awhile they were separated and placed under arrest. It was discovered that one of them had received an ugly, though not dangerous, wound in his side, while the other (our man) had the tendons of his left wrist severed. The men were taken away and the dance proceeded as orderly as before. We now had only two boatmen left. In discussing the matter at home a year later a member of our party remarked that "it was a great pity that the whole bunch wasn't put out of commission; then we would have returned to Tampico, and from there home." One of the natives very courteously invited us to get up and take part in the dance, but after the episode just mentioned we decided not to take a chance.

Our boatmen spent all the next day in fruitless endeavor to secure another helper, and we did not start until the day after at about nine o'clock—a needless delay of forty-two hours; but they were apparently no more concerned than if it had been ten minutes. We were learning to measure time with an elastic tape. Ober complains of the poor traveling facilities in Mexico, and says that "in five days' diligent travel" he accomplished but 220 miles. We had been out longer than that and had not covered twenty miles.

The wind remained contrary all day, as usual, and having but two men, our progress—or lack of progress—was becoming painful. Our provisions, too, were exhausted, and we were reduced to the regular Mexican fare of dried beef and boiled rice. We took a hand at the paddles, but our execution was clumsy and the work uncongenial. Someone suggested that in order to make our discomfiture complete it ought to rain for a day or two, but the boatman reassured us upon this point, saying that it never rained there at that season of the year,—about the only statement they made which was verified by facts. Having made but little progress that day, we held a consultation after our supper of dried beef and rice, and decided that the order of procedure would have to be changed. The wind had ceased and the mosquitoes attacked us in reinforced numbers. We were forced to remain in a much cramped position aboard the boat on top of the cargo, because every time we attempted to stretch our legs on shore we got covered with wood-ticks. It occurred to some of us to wonder what there could possibly be in the whole Republic that would compensate us for such annoyance and privation, and even if we should happen to find anything desirable in that remote district, how could we get in to it or get anything out from it? Certainly none of us had any intention of ever repeating the trip for any consideration. Thus far we had not seen a rubber-tree, vanilla-vine, coffee-tree, or anything else that we would accept as a gift.

Next morning we went over to a nearby hut, and our interpreter calling in at the door asked of the woman inside if we could get some breakfast. "*No hay*" (none here) said she, not even looking up from her work of grinding corn for *tortillas*. He then asked if we could get a cup of hot coffee, to which she again replied "*No hay*." In response to a further inquiry if we could get some hot *tortillas* he got the same "*No hay*," although at that moment there was one baking over the fire and at least a dozen piled up on a low bench, which, in lieu of a table, stood near the fireplace,—which consisted of a small excavation in the dirt floor in the center of the room. The fire was made in this, and the *tortillas* baked on a piece of heavy sheetiron resting on four stones. The interpreter said that we were hungry and had plenty of money to pay for breakfast, but the only reply he got was the same as at first. We therefore returned to the boat and breakfasted on boiled rice and green peppers, the dried beef strips having given out. Soon after our meal I had a severe chill, followed by high fever. Of course we all feared that it was the beginning of smallpox or malaria, or both. Another member of the party was suffering from a racking headache and dizziness, which, he declared, were the first symptoms of smallpox. There was no doctor nearer than Tuxpam or Tampico. The aspect was therefore gloomy enough from any point of view.

We made but little progress during the day. That night after going over the various phases of the situation and fighting mosquitoes—which would bite through our garments at any point where they happened to alight—with no prospect of any rest during the entire night, we found ourselves wrought up to such a mutinous state of mind that it appeared inevitable that something must be done, and that quickly. We directed our interpreter to awaken the owner of the boat and explain the facts to him, which he did. He told him that we had become desperate and that if not landed in Tuxpam in forty-eight hours we purposed putting both him and his man ashore, dumping the cargo, and taking the boat back to Tampico; that we would not be fooled with any longer, and that if he offered any resistance both he and his man would be ejected by main force. The interpreter was a tall, powerful man, standing six feet and two inches in his stocking feet, and had a commanding voice. He had spent several years on the Mexican frontier along the Rio Grande, and understood the Mexicans thoroughly. He needed only the suggestion from us in order to lay the law down to them in a manner not to be mistaken for jesting. This he did for at least ten minutes with scarcely a break of sufficient duration to catch his breath. The boatman, thinking that we were of easy-going, good-natured dispositions, had been quite indifferent to our remonstrances, but he was now completely overwhelmed with astonishment at this sudden outburst. He begged to be given another trial, and said he would not make another stop, except to rest at night, until we reached Tuxpam. We passed a sleepless night with the mosquitoes, frogs, cranes, pelicans, ducks—and perhaps a dozen other varieties of insects and waterfowl—all buzzing, quacking and squawking in unison on every side. In the morning my physical condition was not improved. A little after noon we approached a small settlement on the border of the lake, and stopped to see if we could obtain some medicine and provisions. Our interpreter found what seemed to be the principal man of the place, who took us into his house and provided us with a very good dinner and a couple of quart bottles of Madeira. I had partaken of no food for nearly thirty-six hours, and was unable now to eat anything. We explained to him about the smallpox episode and he agreed that I had all the customary symptoms of the disease. I wrote a message to be despatched by courier to Tampico and from there cabled home, but on second thought it seemed unwise to disturb my family when it was utterly impossible for any of them to reach me speedily, so I tore it up. We arranged for a canoe and four men to start that night and hurry us back to Tampico with all possible speed. The member of our party who had been suffering with headache and dizziness had eaten a hearty dinner, and having had a few glasses of Madeira he was indifferent as to which way he went. During the afternoon I slept for several hours and about seven o'clock awoke, feeling much better. Not desiring to be the cause of abandoning the trip, I had them postpone the return to Tampico until morning. Meanwhile we paid off our boatman, as we had determined to proceed no further with him under any conditions. He remained over night, however. In the morning I felt much better and the fever had left me. We decided to change our plans for return, and to go "on to Tuxpam;" in fact this had now become our watchword. We had had enough of travel by water, and finding a man who claimed to know the route overland we bargained with him to furnish us with four horses and to act as guide, the price to be $100. He also took along an extra guide. The distance, he said, was seventy-five miles, and that we would cover it in twenty-four hours. The highest price that a man could ordinarily claim for his time was fifty cents per day, and the rental of a horse was the same. Allowing the men double pay for night-travel each of them would earn $1.50, and the same returning, making in all $6 for the men; and allowing the same for six horses, their hire would amount to $18, or $24 in all. We endeavored to reason him down, but he was cunning enough to appreciate the urgency of our needs, and wouldn't reduce the price a penny.

It is worthy of note that in this part of the country there is no fixed value to anything when dealing with foreigners. If you ask a native the price of an article, or a personal service, he will very adroitly measure the pressure of your need and will always set the figure at the absolute maximum of what he thinks you would pay, with no regard whatever for the value of the article or service to be given in exchange. If you need a horse quickly and are obliged to have it at any cost, the price is likely to be four times its value. In bartering with the natives it is wise to assume an air of utter indifference as to whether you trade or not. I once gave out notice that I wanted a good saddle-horse, and next morning when I got up there were seventeen standing at my front door, all for sale, but at prices ranging from two to five times their value. I dismissed them all, saying that I didn't need a horse at the time, and a few days later bought the best one of the lot for exactly one quarter of the original asking-price. We were told in Tampico of a recent case where an American traveler employed a man to take his trunk from the hotel to the depot, a distance of less than half a mile, without agreeing upon a price, and the man demanded $10 for the service, which the traveler refused to pay, as the regular and well-established price was but twenty-five cents. The trunk was held and the American missed his train. The case was taken to court and the native won,—the judge holding that the immediate necessity of getting the trunk to the station in time to catch the train justified the charge, especially in that it was for a personal service. The native had been cunning enough to carry the trunk on his back instead of hauling it with his horse and wagon, which stood at the front door of the hotel. The traveler was detained four days in trying the suit, and his lawyer charged him $50 for services. In these parts it is therefore always well to make explicit agreements on prices in advance, especially for personal service to be performed.

In purchasing goods in large quantities one is always expected to pay proportionately more, because they reason that the greater your needs the more urgent they are. I discovered the truth of this statement when purchasing some oranges at the market-place in Tampico. The price was three cents for four oranges. I picked up twelve and gave the man nine cents, but he refused it and asked me for two reals, or twenty-five cents. I endeavored to reason with him, by counting the oranges and the money back and forth, that at the rate of four for three cents, a dozen would come to *medio y quartilla* (nine cents), and nearly wore the skin off the oranges in the process of demonstration; but it was of no use. Finally I took four, and handing him three cents took four more, paying three cents each time until I had completed the dozen. I put them in my valise and left him still counting the money and remonstrating.

We agreed to the extortionate demand of $100 for the hire of the horses and men, only on condition that we were to be furnished with ample provisions for the trip. Leaving our baggage with the boat to be delivered at Tuxpam we started on our horseback journey just after sunset, expecting to reach Tuxpam by sunset next day. The trail led through brush and weeds for several miles, and in less than ten minutes we were covered with wood-ticks from head to foot. Shortly after nightfall we entered a dense forest where the branches closed overhead with such compactness that we couldn't distinguish the movement of our hands immediately before our eyes. The interpreter called to the guide in front and asked if there were any wild animals in these woods; in response we received the cheering intelligence that there were many large panthers and tigers, and that further on along the coast there were lions. After that we momentarily expected to be pounced upon by a hungry tiger or panther from some overhanging bough. The path was crooked, poorly defined, and very rugged. Our faces were frequently raked by the branches of trees and brush, and the blackness seemed to intensify as we progressed. We loosened the reins and allowed the horses to take their course in single file. The guide in front kept up a weird sort of yodling cry which must have penetrated the forest more than a mile. It was a cry of extreme lonesomeness, and is said by the natives to ward off evil spirits and wild animals. I can well understand the foundation for such a belief, particularly in regard to the animals. The pestiferous wood-ticks were annoying us persistently, and it looked as though we had changed for the worse in leaving the boat. At length we came out into the open along the Gulf, and traveled several miles down the coast by the water's edge. It was in the wooded district at our right along here that the lions were so abundant, but I have my doubts if there was a lion, or tiger, or panther anywhere within a mile of us at any time. In my weakened physical condition the exertion was proving too strenuous, and at three o'clock in the morning we all stopped, tied the horses at the edge of the thicket and lay down for a nap beside a large log that had been washed ashore on the sandy beach. The natives assured us that the lions were less likely to eat us if we remained out in the open. A stiff breeze blowing from off the water whirled the dry sand in eddies all along the beach. We nestled behind the log to escape the wind and sand, and in a few minutes were all fast asleep. When we awoke a couple of hours later we were almost literally buried in sand. The wag of the party said it would be an inexpensive burial, and that he didn't intend ever to move an inch from the position in which he lay.

Unaccustomed as we were to horseback riding, it required the most Spartanlike courage to mount our horses again. After going a few miles it came time for breakfast and our interpreter asked one of the guides to prepare the meal. He responded by reaching down into a small bag hanging at his saddle-horn and pulling out four *tortillas*, one for each of us. This was the only article of food they offered us.

It may be explained that the *tortilla* (pronounced torteeya) is the most common article of food in Mexico. It is common in two different senses,— in that it is the cheapest and least palatable food known, and also that it is more generally used than any other food there. In appearance the *tortilla* resembles our pancake, except that it is thinner, tougher, and usually larger around. The size varies from four to seven inches in width, and the thickness from an eighth to a quarter of an inch. It is made of corn, moistened in limewater in order to remove the hulls, then laid on the flat surface of a *metate* (a stone-slab prepared for the purpose), and ground to a thick doughy substance by means of a round stone-bar held horizontally with one hand at each end and rubbed up and down the netherstone, washboard fashion. The women usually do this work, and grind only as much at a time as may be required for the meal. The dough—which contains no seasoning of any kind—not even salt—is pressed and patted into thin cakes between the palms of the hand, and laid on a griddle or piece of sheetiron (stoves being seldom seen) over a fire to bake. They are frequently served with black beans—another very common article of food in Mexico—and by tearing them into small pieces they are made to serve the purpose of knives, forks and spoons in conveying food to the mouth,—the piece of *tortilla* always being deposited in the mouth with the food which it conveys. Among the poorer classes the *tortilla* is frequently the only food taken for days and perhaps weeks at a time. It is never baked crisp, but is cooked just enough to change the color slightly. When served hot, with butter—an *extremely* rare article in the rural districts—it is rather agreeable to the taste, but when cold it becomes very tough and in taste it resembles the sole of an old rubber shoe.

Such was the food that was offered us in fulfillment of the promise to supply us with an abundance of good provisions for the journey. I had eaten scarcely anything for three days, and with the improvement in my physical condition my appetite was becoming unmanageable. We found that it would probably be impossible to obtain food until we reached Tamiahua, a small town about thirty miles down the coast. It would be tiresome and useless to dwell further upon the monotony of that day's travel along the sands of the barren coast, with nothing to eat since the afternoon before. Suffice it to say that we all were still alive when we arrived at Tamiahua at about three o'clock in the afternoon. Meanwhile we had been planning how best to get even with the Mexicans for having bled us and then starved us. Fortunately, we had paid only half the sum in advance, and the remaining half would at least procure us a good meal. We went to a sort of inn kept by an accommodating native who promised to get up a good dinner for us. We told him to get everything he could think of that we would be likely to enjoy, to spare no expense in providing it, and to spread the table for six.

Tamiahua is situated on the coast, cut off from the mainland by a small body of water through which the small freight boats pass in plying between Tampico and Tuxpam. There happened to be a boat at the wharf, just arrived from Tampico with a load of groceries destined for Tuxpam. The innkeeper suggested that there might be some American goods aboard, and we all went down to interview the boatman. He informed us that the cargo was consigned to a grocer in Tuxpam and that he couldn't sell anything, but when our interpreter slipped a couple of silver *pesos* (dollars) into his palm he told us to pick out anything we wanted. We took a five-pound can of American butter, at $1 a pound, an imported ham at fifty cents a pound, a ten-pound tin box of American crackers at fifty cents a pound, four boxes of French sardines, two cans of evaporated cream, and a selection of canned goods, the bill amounting in all to $22.25. This was all taken to the inn and opened up. The innkeeper was instructed to keep what we couldn't eat. The butter was so strong that he kept the most of that, with more than half of the crackers. At five o'clock we were served with a dinner of fried chicken, fried ham and eggs, canned baked beans, bread and butter, coffee, and native fruit. The two guides were invited to sit down with us to what was doubtless the most sumptuous feast ever set before them. After dinner we called for a dozen of the best cigars that the town afforded, and two were handed to each one, including the guides. After lighting our cigars we called for the bill of the entire amount, which, including the sum of $22.25 for the boatman, came to $38.50. We called the innkeeper into the room, counted out $50 on the table, and paid him $38.50 for the dinner and the boatman's bill; then gave him $5 extra for himself, while the remaining $6.50 was handed to the head guide. He almost collapsed with astonishment, and wondered what he had done to deserve such a generous honorarium; but his amazement was increased ten-fold when the interpreter informed him that this was the balance due him. A heated argument ensued between them, and the guide drawing his machete attempted to make a pass at the interpreter, with the remark that he would kill every *gringo* (a vulgar term applied to English-speaking people by the Mexicans in retaliation for the term *greaser*) in the place. The innkeeper pounced upon him with the quickness of a cat and pinioned his arms behind him. His companion seeing that he was subdued made no move. The innkeeper called for a rope and in less than five minutes the belligerent Mexican was bound hand and foot and was being carried to the lockup. The interpreter explained the whole matter to the innkeeper, who sided with us, of course. The effect of the five-dollar tip was magical. He went to the judge and pleaded our case so eloquently that that dignitary called upon us in the evening and apologized on behalf of his countrymen for the indignity, assuring us incidentally that the offender would be dealt with according to the law. We presented him with an American five-dollar gold piece as a souvenir. He insisted that we remain over night as his guests, and in the morning piloted us through the village. The first place visited was the cathedral, a large structure standing in the center of the principal street. Its seating capacity was perhaps five times greater than that of any other building in the village. It contained a number of pieces of beautiful old statuary, and on the walls were many magnificent old paintings, of enormous dimensions, with splendid frames. They are said to have been secretly brought to this obscure out-of-the-way place from the City of Mexico during the French invasion, but for what reason they were never removed seems a mystery.

A *fiesta* was in progress in honor of the birthday of some saint, and it was impossible to get anyone to take us to Tuxpam, only a few miles distant. We desired to continue via the *laguna*, and engaged two men to take us in a sort of gondola, with the understanding that we should leave just after sunset. We gave the men a dollar apiece in advance, as they wished to purchase a few articles of food, etc., for the journey, and they were to meet us at the inn at sunset. Neither of them appeared at the appointed time, and in company with the innkeeper we went in search of them. In the course of half an hour we found one of the men behind a hut, drunk, and asleep. He had drank a whole quart of *aguardiente* and the empty bottle lay at his side. We left him and went to the boat, where we found the other man stretched out full length in the bottom with a half-filled bottle beside him. We concluded to start out and to put the man at the paddle as soon as he became sufficiently sober. The innkeeper directed us as best he could and we pushed off from the shore about an hour after nightfall, expecting to reach Tuxpam by eight o'clock next morning. We were told to paddle out across the lake about a mile to the opposite shore, where there was a channel leading into a large lake beyond. The water was very shallow most of the way, and filled with marshgrass and other vegetation, which swarmed with a great variety of waterfowl. Disturbed by our approach they kept up a constant quacking, squawking and screeching on all sides, which, reverberating on the still night-air, made the scene dismal enough. There was a *baile* in progress near the shore in the village and as we paddled along far out in the lake we could see the glimmer of the lights reflected along the surface of the water and could hear the dance-music distinctly. When we had gotten well out into the lake the drunken man in the bottom of the boat waked up and inquired where he was and where we were taking him. Seeing the lights in the distance and hearing the music he suddenly remembered that he had promised to take his girl to the dance, and demanded that he be taken back to shore. Upon being refused he jumped out into the water and declared that he would wade back. We had great difficulty in getting him back into the boat and came near capsizing in the operation. The ducking he got sobered him up considerably and at length we got him at the helm with the paddle and told him to head for the mouth of the channel. He neared the shore to the right of the channel and following along near the water's edge was within a quarter of a mile of the village before we realized what his trick was. The interpreter took the paddle away from him and told him of the dire consequences that would follow if he didn't settle down and behave himself. After turning the boat around and following along the shore for half a mile he promised to take us to Tuxpam if we would agree to get him another bottle of *aguardiente* there and also a present with which to make peace with his girl. Upon being assured that we would do this he seemed quite contented and set to work in earnest. As we entered the narrow channel a large dog ran out from a nearby hut, and approaching the boat threatened to devour us all. Provoked at this interference the Mexican made a swish at him in the dark with the paddle, but missing the dog he struck the ground with such violence that the handle of the paddle broke off near the blade, and both Mexican and paddle tumbled headlong into the water with a splash. This provoked the dog to still greater savagery, and jumping from the bank into the boat he attacked the interpreter with the ferocity of a tiger. He was immediately shot and dumped into the water. Meanwhile our gondolier had clambered up on the bank and the two pieces of the paddle had floated off in the darkness. What to do was a serious question. The native at the hut had probably been aroused by the shot and was likely to come down on us with more ferocity than the dog. We could not therefore appeal to him for another paddle. It was so dark that we could scarcely see one another in the boat, and it was exceedingly fortunate that none of the party was shot instead of the dog. While we were debating the various phases of our predicament the Mexican—who had now become quite sober after his second sousing—unsheathed his machete and cut a pole, with the aid of which he soon had us a safe distance down the channel. A few miles further on we got out at a hut by the side of the channel and bought a paddle, for which we paid three times its value.

The channels from here on were generally overhung on both sides with brush and the boughs of trees, and the darkness was so intense that it was impossible to distinguish any object at a distance of three feet. The man at the paddle set up the same doleful yodling cry that we had heard in the woods, and continued it at intervals all through the night. He advised us to be careful not to allow our hands to hang over the edge of the boat, as the channel abounded with alligators. As a matter of fact, I doubt if there was an alligator within miles of us. The native was doubtless sincere in his statement, because he had perhaps heard others say that there were alligators there. The story of the lions, tigers and panthers in the woods along the coast was also undoubtedly a myth which like many other sayings had become a popular belief from frequent repetition. The same is true of dozens of tales one hears in Mexico, and about Mexico when at home. For example, the fabulous stories about the vast fortunes to be made in planting vanilla, rubber trees and coffee; but I shall treat of these matters in their proper place further on.

We finally arrived at Tuxpam in the morning at nine o'clock. As I reflected upon the experiences of the past two weeks I shuddered at the very thought of returning. It is doubtful if all the riches in this tropical land could have tempted me again to undergo the tortures and anxiety of body and mind that fell to my portion on that journey. It was an epoch long to be remembered.

Tuxpam is a pleasant sanitary town of perhaps five thousand inhabitants situated on the banks of the beautiful Tuxpam River a few miles inland from the coast. The town is built on both sides of the river, which carries off all the refuse and drainage to the ocean below. This being a narrative of experiences rather than a history of towns and villages, I have purposely refrained from long-drawn-out topographical descriptions. The reader is doubtless familiar with the general details of the crude architecture that characterizes all Mexican villages and cities, and a detailed recital of this would be a needless repetition of well-known facts, for there is a monotonous sameness in the appearance of all Mexican towns and villages. For the purpose of this narrative it matters little to the reader whether the people of Tuxpam are all Aztecs, Spaniards, French or Indians, though in point of fact they consist of a sprinkling of all of these. Tuxpam itself is simply a characteristic Mexican town, but it should be here permanently recorded that it has within its precincts one of the most adorable women to whom the Lord ever gave the breath of life: Mrs. Messick, the widow of the former American consul, is a native Mexican of ebony hue, but with a heart as large and charitable and true as ever beat in a human breast. She is far from prepossessing in appearance, and yet to look upon her amiable features and to converse with her in her broken English is a treat long to be remembered. Her commodious home is a veritable haven for every orphan, cripple, blind or otherwise infirm person that comes within her range of vision, and her retinue of servants, with herself at their head, are constantly engaged in cooking, washing and otherwise caring for the comforts and alleviating the sufferings of those unfortunates who are her special charges. She furnishes an illustrious example of the spirit of a saint inhabiting a bodily form, and it is almost worth the trip to Mexico to find that the native race can boast a character of such noble instincts.

Arriving at this picturesque town we went at once to the hotel. This hostelry consisted of a chain of rooms built upon posts about nine feet from the ground, and extending around the central market-place. There is a veranda around the inside of the square, from which one may obtain a good view of the market. The stands, or stalls, are around the outer edge under the tier of rooms, while in the center men and women sit on the ground beside piles of a great variety of fresh vegetables and other perishable articles for household use. There is perhaps no better selection of vegetables to be found in any market in America than we saw here.

The partitions dividing the tier of rooms were very thin and extended up only about two-thirds of the way from the floor to the ceiling, so there was an air-space connecting all the rooms overhead. One could hear every word spoken in the adjoining room on either side. The furniture consisted of a cot-bed, a wash-stand and a chair. We each procured a room, and as we looked them over and noted the open space overhead, someone remarked that "it would be a great place for smallpox." Having had no sleep the night before, and being very tired after sitting in a cramped position all night in the boat, we retired shortly after reaching town. At about four o'clock in the afternoon I was awakened by a vigorous pounding at my door, and my two companions, who were outside, shouted, "*Get up quick!* there is a case of smallpox in the next room!" I jumped up quickly and in my dazed condition put on what clothing I could readily lay my hands on, and snatching up my shoes and coat ran out on the veranda. After getting outside I discovered that I had gotten into my trousers hind side before and had left my hat, collar, shirt and stockings behind, but did not return for them. We all beat a hasty retreat around the veranda to the opposite side, of the court, or square, and the people in the market-place below having heard the pounding on the door, and seeing me running along the veranda in my *déshabillé* concluded that the place was afire. Someone gave the alarm of fire, and general pandemonium ensued. The women-peddlers and huxsters in the market hastily gathered up such of their effects as they could carry and ran out of the inclosure into the street. In remarkable contrast to the usual solicitude and thoughtfulness of motherhood, I saw one woman gather up a piece of straw-matting with about fifty pounds of dried shrimp and scurry out into the street, leaving her naked baby sitting howling on the bare ground. Vegetables and all sorts of truck were hurriedly dumped into bags and carried out. Happily this episode occurred in the afternoon when there was comparatively little doing, and very few pedestrians in the place; for had it happened in the early morning when all the people are gathered to purchase household necessities for the day, a serious panic would have been inevitable. About this time our interpreter appeared, and three soldiers in white uniforms came rushing up to us and enquired where the fire was. My companions explained to the soldiers, through the interpreter, that it was only a practical joke they had played on me. It now became my turn to laugh, for they were both placed under arrest and taken before the magistrate, charged with disturbing the peace and starting a false alarm of fire. When the interpreter explained the matter to the magistrate that official lost his dignity for a moment and laughed outright. He was a good-natured old fellow (an unusual characteristic, I understand, among Mexican magistrates) and appreciated the joke even more than I did. He recovered his dignity and composure long enough to give us an impressive warning not to play any more such pranks, and dismissed the case.

Our baggage did not arrive until five days later, and was soaking wet, as the boatman said he had encountered a gale in which he had barely escaped inundation.

There was an American merchant in Tuxpam by the name of Robert Boyd, whose store was the headquarters of all Americans, both resident and traveling. Had we talked with Mr. Boyd before going to Mexico there would have been no occasion for writing this narrative. He was an extremely alert trader and in his thirty years' residence, by conducting a general store and trafficking in such native products as *chicle* (gum,—pronounced chickly), hides, cedar, rubber and vanilla, which he shipped in small quantities to New York, he had accumulated about $50,000 (Mexican). We had expected to make on an average that sum for every day we spent in Mexico, and were astonished that a man of his commanding appearance and apparent ability should be running a little store and doing a small three-penny business. Three months later we would have concluded that any American who could make fifty thousand dollars by trading with Mexicans for thirty years is highly deserving of a bronze monument on a conspicuous site. For clever trading in a small way, the Mexican is as much ahead of the average Yankee as our present methods of printing are ahead of those employed in Caxton's time. They are exceedingly cunning traders and will thrive where even the Italian fruit-vender would starve.

When we informed Mr. Boyd that we had come in search of vanilla, rubber and coffee lands he must have felt sorry for us; in fact he admitted as much to me a few months later when I knew him better. With his characteristic courtesy, however, he told us of several places that we might visit. We learned for the first time that the three industries require entirely different soils and altitudes. For coffee-land he recommended that we go up the Tuxpam River to what was known as the *Mesa* (high table-lands) district, while for vanilla-land he recommended either Misantla or Papantla, further down the coast; and rubber trees, he said, could be grown with moderate success in certain localities around Tuxpam. He did not discourage us, because it was not consonant with his business interests to dissuade American enterprise and investments there, no matter how ill-advised the speculation might be. Others before us had come and gone; some had left their money, while others had been wise enough to get back home with it, and stay there. Some investors had returned wiser, but never was one known to return richer. All this, however, we did not learn until later. We made several short journeys on horseback, but found no lands that seemed suitable for our purposes. There were too many impediments in the vanilla industry,—not least among which was the alacrity with which the natives will steal the vanilla-beans as fast as they mature. In fact, a common saying there is, "catch your enemy in your vanilla-patch,"—for you would be justified in shooting him at sight, even though he happened there by accident. It requires a watchman to every few dozen vines (which are grown among the trees) and then for every few watchmen it needs another watchman to keep an observing eye on them. Again, the vanilla country is uncomfortably near the yellow fever zone.

As to rubber, we found very few trees in bearing, and the few scattering ones we saw that had been "tapped," or rather "gashed," in order to bleed them of their milk, were slowly dying. True, the native method of extracting the milk from the trees was crude, but they did not appear hardy.

One of the principal articles of export from this section is chicle. The reader may not be aware that a great deal of our chewing-gum comes from this part of Mexico, and that it is a thoroughly pure and wholesome vegetable product. The native *Chiclero* is the best paid man among the common laborers in Mexico. Tying one end of a long rope around his waist he climbs up the tree to the first large limb—perhaps from thirty to sixty feet—and throwing the other end of the rope over the branch lets himself down slowly by slipping the rope through his left hand, while with the right hand he wields a short bladed machete with which he chops gashes in the tree at an angle of about forty-five degrees, which leading into a little groove that he makes all the way down, conducts the sap down to the base of the tree, where it is carried into a basin or trough by means of a leaf inserted in a gash in the tree near the ground. This is a very hazardous undertaking and requires for its performance a dexterous, able-bodied man. A single misstroke may sever the rope and precipitate the operator to the ground. In this way a great number of men are killed every year. The sap is a thick, white creamy substance, and is boiled down in vats the same as the sap from the maple tree. When it reaches a certain thickness or temperature it is allowed to cool, after which it is made up into chunks or squares weighing from ten to forty pounds each. It is then carried to market on mule-back. The crude chicle has a delightful flavor, which is entirely destroyed by the gum-manufacturers, who mix in artificial flavors, with a liberal percentage of sugar. If the gum-chewer could obtain crude chicle with its delicious native flavor he (or she) would never be content to chew the article as prepared for the trade.

Rubber is produced in the same way as chicle, and the milk from the rubber tree is scarcely distinguishable, except in flavor, from that of the chicle-producing tree. The latter, however, grows to much greater size and is more hardy. It abounds throughout the forests in the lowlands. The native rubber trees die after being gashed a few times, and those we saw in bearing were very scattering. You might not see a dozen in a day's travel.

The easiest way to make money on rubber trees is to write up a good elastic article on the possibilities of the industry, form a ten or twenty million dollar corporation and sell the stock to the uninitiated,—if there are any such left. It would be a debatable question with me, however, which would be the more attractive from an investment point of view,—stock in a rubber company in Mexico, or one in Mars. Both would have their advantages; the one in Mexico would possess the advantage of closer proximity, while the one in Mars would have the advantage of being so far away that one could never go there to be disillusioned. The chances for legitimate returns would be about the same in both places. It seems a pity that any of those persons who ever bought stock in bogus Mexican development companies should have suffered the additional humiliation of afterwards going down there to see what they had bought into.

It is surprising that up to the present time no one has appeared before the credulous investing public with a fifty-million dollar chicle corporation, for here is a valuable commodity that grows wild in the woods almost everywhere, and a highly imaginative writer could devote a whole volume to the unbounded possibilities of making vast fortunes in this industry.

While I was in Mexico a friend sent me some advertising matter of one of these development companies that was paying large dividends on its enormous capital stock from the profits on pineapples and coffee, when in point of fact there was not a coffee-tree on its place, and it was producing scarcely enough pineapples to supply the caretaker's family.

In regard to coffee, we found that some American emigration company appeared to be making a legitimate effort to test the productivity of that staple, and had sent a number of thrifty American families into Mexico and settled them at the *mesa*, several miles inland from Tuxpam. They had cleared up a great deal of land and put out several thousand coffee-plants. There are many reasons why this crop cannot be extensively and profitably raised in this part of Mexico,—and for that matter, I presume, in any other part. Foremost among the many obstacles is the labor problem. The native help is not only insufficient, but is utterly unreliable. It is at picking-time that the greatest amount of help is required, and even if it were possible to rely upon the laborers, and there were enough of them, there would not be sufficient work to keep them between the harvest-seasons. It would be totally impracticable to import laborers; the expense and the climate would both be prohibitive. Again, the price of labor here has increased greatly of late years, without a corresponding appreciation in the price of coffee.

Neither vanilla, coffee nor rubber had ever been profitably raised in large quantities and we therefore decided that under the existing circumstances and hindrances we would dismiss these three articles from further consideration.

If we had been content to return home and charge our trip to experience account, all would have been well,—but we pursued our investigations along other lines. The possibilities of the tobacco industry claimed our attention for awhile—it also claimed a considerable amount of money from one of my companions. Someone (perhaps the one who had the land for sale) had recently discovered that the ground in a certain locality was peculiarly suited to the growth of fine tobacco, which could be raised at low cost and sold at fabulous prices. We learned that a large tract of land in this singularly-favored district was for sale; so thither we went in search of information. The soil was rich and heavily wooded; it looked as though it might produce tobacco or almost anything else. I neither knew nor cared anything about tobacco-raising and the place did not therefore interest me in the least. One of my companions, however, had been doing a little figuring on his own account, and had calculated that he could buy this place, hire a foreman to run it, put in from five to eight hundred acres of tobacco that year, and that the place would pay for itself and be self-sustaining the second year. By the third year he would have a thousand acres in tobacco, and the profits would be enormous. It would not require his personal attention, and he could send monthly remittances from home for expenses, and probably come down once a year on a *pleasure trip*. Parenthetically, by way of assurance to the reader that the man had not entirely lost his reason, I may say that we learned in Tuxpam that of all routes and modes of travel to that place we had selected by far the worst; that the best way was to take a Ward Line Steamer from New York to Havana, and from there around by Progreso, Campeche, and up the coast to Vera Cruz, thence to Tuxpam. From Tuxpam the steamers go to Tampico, then back to Havana and New York. However, one cannot count with certainty on landing at Tuxpam, as the steamers are obliged to stop outside the bar and the passengers and cargo have to be lightered over. The steamers often encounter bad weather along the coast, and it frequently happens that passengers and freight destined for Tuxpam are carried on up to Tampico.

My friend had gotten his money easily and was now unconsciously planning a scheme for spending it with equal facility. The more we tried to dissuade him the more convinced he was of the feasibility of the plan. We argued that no one had ever made any money in tobacco there, and that it was an untried industry. He said that made no difference; it was because they didn't know how to raise tobacco. He would import a practical tobacco-man from Cuba—which he finally did, under a guarantee of $200 a month for a year—and that he would show the Mexicans how to raise tobacco. He bought the place, arranged through a friend in Cuba for an expert tobacco-raiser, and sent couriers through the country to engage a thousand men for chopping and clearing. He was cautioned against attempting to clear too much land, as it was very late. The rainy season begins in June, and after that it is impossible to burn the clearings over. The method of clearing land here is to cut down the trees and brush early in the spring, trim off the branches and let them lie until thoroughly dry. In felling a forest and chopping up the brush and limbs it forms a layer over the entire area, sometimes five or six feet deep. Under the hot sun of April and May, during which time it rarely rains more than a slight sprinkle, this becomes very dry and highly inflammable. Early in June the fires are set, and at this season the whole country around is filled with a hazy atmosphere. The heat from the bed of burning tinder is so intense that most of the logs are consumed and many of the stumps are killed; thus preventing them from sprouting. Every foul seed in the ground is destroyed and for a couple of years scarcely any cultivation is required.

Our would-be tobacco-raiser paid no heed to advice or words of warning; he was typical of most Americans who seek to make fortunes in Mexico,—they have great difficulty in getting good advice, but it is ten times more difficult to get them to follow it. You rarely obtain trustworthy information from your own countrymen who have investments there, for the chances are fifty to one that they are anxious to sell out, and will paint everything in glowing hues in the hope that they may unload their burdens on you. Even if they have nothing to sell, they are none the less optimistic, for they like to see you invest your money. Wretched conditions are in a measure mitigated by companionship; in other words, "Misery loves company."

Hereafter I shall refer to the man who bought the tobacco land as Mr. A., and to my other companion as Mr. B.

Mr. A. was delayed in getting his foreman and had the customary difficulty in hiring help. Three hundred men was all he could muster at first, and they were secured only by paying a liberal advance of twenty-five per cent. over the usual wages. They began cutting timber about the 28th of April,—the season when this work should have been finished, and continued until the rainy season commenced, when scarcely any of the clearing had been burned; and after the rains came it was impossible to start a fire, so the whole work of felling upwards of four hundred acres of forest was abandoned. Every stub and stump seemed to shoot up a dozen sprouts, and growing up through the thick layer of brush, branches and logs, they formed a network that challenged invasion by man or beast. The labor was therefore all lost and the tobacco project abandoned in disgust.

I was told by one of the oldest inhabitants—past ninety—that it had never once failed to rain on San Juan's (Saint John's) Day, the 24th of June. Sometimes the rainy season begins a little earlier, and occasionally a little later, but that day never passes without bringing at least a light shower. Of course it was in accord with my friend's run of luck that this should be the year when the rainy season began prematurely; but the truth of the matter is, it was about the most fortunate circumstance that could have occurred; for as it turned out he lost only the money laid out for labor, together with the excess price paid for the land above what it was worth; whereas, had everything gone well he was likely to have lost many thousands of dollars more.

In the meantime I had been looking the field over industriously, and had concluded that the sugar and cattle industries promised the surest and greatest returns. I heard of a ranch, with sugar-plantation, for sale up in the Tuxpam valley. It was owned by an American who had occupied it forty-seven years, during which time he had made enough to live comfortably and educate two sons in American schools. He was well past seventy and wished to retire from the cares of active business,—which I regarded as a justifiable excuse for selling. We visited the place and found the only American-built house we had seen since leaving home. The place was in a fairly good state of repair, though the pasture lands and canefields had been allowed to deteriorate. The whole place was for sale, including cattle, mules, wagons, sugar-factory, tenement houses, machinery and growing crops; in fact, everything went. The price asked appeared so low that I was astonished at the owner's modesty in estimating its value. I accepted his offer on the spot, paying a small sum down to bind the bargain,—fearing that he would change his mind. It was not long, however, before I changed my estimate of his modesty, and marveled at his boldness in having the courage to ask the price he did. On our way back to town my companions argued that I was foolish to try to make money in sugar or cattle raising; that there was no nearby market for the cattle, and that the Cuban sugar was produced so abundantly and so cheaply that there would be no profit in competing with it in the American market. This was perfectly sound logic, as testified to by later experiences, but it fell upon deaf ears. I had been inoculated with the sugar and cattle germ as effectively as my friend had been with the tobacco germ, and could see nothing but profit everywhere. Mr. A. was to have a Cuban tobacco man, and why couldn't I have an experienced Cuban sugar man? I expected to double the magnitude of the canefields, as the foreman—who promised to remain—had declared that this could be done without crowding the capacity of the factory. I would also import some shorthorn cattle from the United States, and figured out that I should need a whole carload of farming implements.

It may be remarked that almost without exception the American visitor here is immediately impressed with the unbounded possibilities of making vast fortunes. The resources of the soil appear almost limitless. The foliage of the trees and shrubs is luxuriant the year round, and the verdure of the pastures and all vegetation is inspiring at all seasons. The climate is delightful, even in midsummer, and with such surroundings and apparent advantages for agricultural pursuits one marvels at the inactivity and seeming stupidity of the natives. After a few months' experience in contending with the multiplicity of pests and perversities that stand athwart the path of progress, and becoming inoculated with the monotony of the tropical climate, one can but wonder that there should be any energy or ambition at all. The tendency of Americans is always to apply American energy and ideas to Mexican conditions, with the result that nothing works harmoniously. The country here is hundreds of years behind our times, and cannot be brought into step with our progressiveness except by degrees. Our modern methods and ideas assimilate with those of Mexico very slowly, if at all. It is almost impossible to develop any one locality or industry independent of the surroundings. The truth is, if you would live comfortably in Mexico (which in these parts is quite beyond human possibility) you must live as Mexicans do, for they are clever enough, and have lived here long enough, to make the best of conditions. If you would farm successfully in Mexico, you must farm precisely as they do, for you will eventually find that there is some well-grounded reason for every common usage; and if you would make money in Mexico, stay away entirely and dismiss the very thought of it. Pure cream cannot be extracted from chalk and water,—though it may look like milk,—because the deficiency of the necessary elements forbids it; no more can fortunes be made in this part of Mexico, because they are not here to be made, as every condition forbids their accumulation. The impoverished condition of the people is such that a large percentage of the families subsist on an average income of less than ten cents a day, silver.

Although the peon class are indigent, lazy and utterly devoid of ambition they are so by virtue of climatic and other conditions that surround them, and of which they can be but the natural outgrowth. The debilitating effects of the climate, and the numberless bodily pests draw so heavily upon human vitality that it is surprising that any one after a year's residence there can muster sufficient energy to work at all. The natives, after a day's labor will throw themselves upon the hard ground and fall asleep, calmly submitting to the attack of fleas and wood-ticks as a martyrdom from which it is useless to attempt to escape. It is a labored and painful existence they lead, and it is not to be wondered at that smallpox, pestilence and death have no terror for them; indeed, they hail these as welcome messengers of relief. When by the pangs of hunger they are driven to the exertion of work they will do a fair day's labor, if kept constantly under the eye of a watchman, or *capitan*, as he is called. One of these is required for about every ten or twelve workmen; otherwise they would do nothing at all. If twenty workmen were sent to the field to cut brush, without designating someone as captain, they would not in the course of the whole day clear a patch large enough to sit down on. The best workmen are the Indians that come down from the upper-country settlements. Upon leaving home they take along about twelve days' rations, usually consisting of black beans and corn ground up together into a thick dough and made into little balls a trifle larger than a hen's egg, and baked in hot ashes. They eat three of these a day,—one for each meal,—and when the supply is exhausted they collect their earnings and return to their homes, no matter how urgent the demand for their continued service may be. In two or three weeks they will return again with another supply of provisions and stay until it is consumed, but no longer. If Thoreau could have seen how modestly these people live he would have learned a lesson in economic living such as he never dreamed of. The frugality of his meagre fare at his Walden pond hermitage would have appeared like wanton luxury by comparison. If the virtue of honesty can be ascribed to any of these laborers the Indians are entitled to the larger share of it. They keep pretty much to themselves and seldom inter-marry or mingle socially with the dusky-skinned Aztecs.

It is difficult to get the natives to work as long as they have a little corn for *tortillas* or a pound of beans in the house. I have known dozens of instances where they would come at daylight in search of a day's work, leaving the whole family at home without a mouthful of victuals. If successful in getting work they would prefer to take their day's pay in corn, and would not return to work again until it was entirely exhausted. Hundreds of times at my ranch men applying for work were so emaciated and exhausted from lack of nourishment that they had to be fed before they were in a fit condition to send to the field.

The basic element of wealth is money, and it is impossible to make an exchange of commodities for money in great quantity where it exists only in small quantity. In other words, if you would make money it is of first importance that you go where there is money. If—as is the case—a man will labor hard from sunrise to sunset in Mexico, and provision himself, for twenty-five cents in gold, it would indicate either a scarcity of gold or a superabundance of willing laborers, and it must be the former, for the latter does not exist. Some have argued that money is to be made in Mexico by producing such articles as may be readily exchanged for American gold, but there are very few articles of merchandise for which we are *obliged* to go to Mexico, and these cost to produce there nearly as much or more than we have to pay for them. For example, a pound of coffee in Mexico costs fifty cents, the equivalent in value to the labor of an able-bodied man for twelve hours. There is some good reason for this condition, else it would not exist. In other words, if it didn't cost the monetary value of twelve hours' work (less the merchant's reasonable profit, of course) to produce a pound of coffee, it would not cost that to buy it there. It does not seem logical, therefore, that it can be produced and sold profitably to a country where a pound of this commodity is equal in value to less than two hours of a man's labor. If it were so easy and profitable to raise coffee, every native might have his own little patch for home use, and possibly a few pounds to sell. In order to be profitable, commodities must be turned out at a low cost and sold at a high cost; but here is a case where some visionary Americans have thought to get rich by working directly against the order of economic and natural laws. I have not consulted statistics to ascertain how the Mexican exports to the United States compare with their imports of our products, but it is a significant fact, as stated at the beginning of this narrative, that the highest premium obtainable for American money is for eastern exchange, used in settling balances for imports of American goods. The needs of the average Mexican are very small beyond the products of his own soil, and if the agricultural exports from their eastern ports were large the merchants would have but little difficulty in purchasing credits on New York, or any important eastern or southern seaport.

I had the good fortune *not* to be able to make any satisfactory arrangement for a practical sugar-maker from Cuba. I was more fortunate than my friend Mr. A., in not having any friend there to look out for me. Thus I saved not only the cost of an expert's services, which, comparatively speaking, would have been a trifling item, but was held up in making the contemplated extensions and improvements until my sugar-fever had subsided and I had regained my normal senses, after which I was quite contented to conduct the place in its usual way with a few slight improvements here and there. I had not in so short a time become quite reconciled, however, to the idea that the place could not be run at a profit; but figured that it could be made to yield me a considerable revenue above expenses, and that it would afford a desirable quartering-place for my family on an occasional tropical visit in winter. After returning home later in the season I induced my family to return with me in the fall and spend a part of the following winter there; and although we experienced the novelty on Christmas-day of standing on our front porch and picking luscious ripe oranges from the trees,—one of which stands at each side of the steps,—I have never again been able to bring my persuasive powers to a point where I could induce them to set foot on Mexican soil. It is largely due to the abhorrence of smallpox, malaria, snakes, scorpions, tarantulas, *garrapatas*, fleas, and a few other minor pests and conditions to which they object. Mosquitoes, however, did not molest us at the ranch.

Once while we were at the ranch my wife was told by one of the servants that there was a woman at the front door to see her. Upon going into the hall she found that the woman had stepped inside and taken a seat near the door. She arose timidly, with a bundle in her arms—which proved to be a babe—and spoke, but Mrs. Harper could not understand a word she said. The maid had entered the hall immediately behind my wife, and, as she spoke both Spanish and English, the woman explained through her that the baby was suffering with smallpox, and that she had heard that there was an American woman there who could cure it. The resultant confusion in the household beggars description. Every time I mention Mexico at home I get a graphic rehearsal of this scene. The poor woman had walked ten miles, carrying her babe, and thought she was doing no harm in bringing it in and sitting down to rest for a moment. She was put into a boat and taken down the river to Tuxpam by one of the men on the place who had already passed through the stages of this disease, and under the treatment of a Spanish physician whom I had met there the child recovered and was sent back home with its mother.

It may be observed that since arriving at Tuxpam I have appeared to neglect my friend Mr. B., but, although so far as this narrative is concerned he has not as yet been much in evidence, he was by far the busiest man in the party. Being the only unmarried man in our company he had not been long in Mexico when he began to busy himself with an industry in which single men hold an unchallenged monopoly, and one that is far more absorbing than vanilla, rubber, coffee, sugar and tobacco all combined. The immediate cause of his diversion was due to a visit that we all made to the large hacienda of a wealthy Spanish gentleman of education and refinement, who had a very beautiful and accomplished daughter but recently returned home with her mother from an extended tour through Europe, following her graduation from a fashionable and well-known ladies' seminary in America. I have made the statement in the foregoing pages that no American fortune-hunter had been known to return home from here richer than when he came, but later on we shall see that this no longer remains a truth. For the present, however, as long as we are now discussing problems of vulgar commerce, we shall leave Mr. B. undisturbed in his more engaging pursuit, and return to his case later.

Next to silver, corn is the staple and standard of value in Mexico, though its price fluctuates widely. Everybody, and nearly every animal, both untamed and domestic, and most of the insects, feed upon this article. It is the one product of the soil that can be readily utilized and converted into cash in any community and at any season. The price is usually high, often reaching upwards of the equivalent of $1 a bushel. It is measured not by the bushel, but by the *fanega*, which weighs 225 pounds. It may appear a strange anomaly that the principal native product should be so high in a soil of such wonderful productivity. An acre of ground will produce from fifty to seventy-five bushels, *twice a year*. It is planted in June as soon as the rains break the long, monotonous dry season which extends through March, April and May, and is harvested early in October; then the same ground is planted again in December for harvesting early in April. The ground requires no plowing and, if recently cleared, no weeding; so all that is necessary to do is to plant the corn and wait for it to mature. It sounds easy and looks easy, but, as with everything else, there are a few obstacles. Corn is planted in rows, about the same distance apart as in America, and is almost universally of the white variety, as this is the best for *tortillas*. The planting is accomplished by puncturing the ground with a hardwood pole, sharpened at one end. The hole is made from four to six inches deep, when the top of the pole is moved from one side to another so that the point loosens up the subsoil and makes an opening at the bottom of the hole the same width as that at the top. The corn is then dropped in and covered with a little dirt which is knocked in by striking the point of the pole gently at the opening. The moisture, however, would cause it to sprout and grow even if not covered at all. The difficulties now begin and continue successively and uninterruptedly at every stage of development to maturity, and even until the corn is finally consumed. The first of these difficulties is in the form of a small red ant which appears in myriads and eats the germ of the kernels as soon as they are planted. When the corn sprouts there is a small cut-worm that attacks it in great numbers. When the sprouts begin to make their appearance above the ground there is a blackbird lying in wait at every hill to pull it up and get the kernel. These birds, which in size are between our crow and blackbird, appear in great numbers and would destroy a ten-acre field of corn in one day if not frightened away. They have long sharp beaks, and insatiable appetites. Following these the army-worm attacks the stalk when knee high, and penetrating it at the top or tassel-end stops its growth and destroys it. These ravages continue until the corn begins to tassel, if any is so fortunate as to reach that stage. When the ears appear another worm works in at the silk, and a little later a small bird resembling our sapsucker puts in his claim to a share in the crop. Beginning at the outer edge of the field and proceeding down the row from one hill to another, he penetrates the husks of almost every ear with his needlelike bill, and the moment the milky substance of the corn is reached the ear is abandoned and another attacked. When punctured in this way the ear withers and dries up without maturing. The succession is then taken up by the parrots and parrakeets, which abound in Mexico. They may be seen in flocks flying overhead or hovering over some field, constantly chattering and squawking, at almost any hour of the day. When the corn begins to mature the raccoons appear from the woods, and entering a field at night they eat and destroy the corn like a drove of hogs. As a means of protection against these pests many of the natives keep a number of dogs, which they tie out around the field at night, and which keep up an almost constant barking and howling. Finally, just as the corn has matured and the kernels are hardening the fall rains begin, and often continue for days and even weeks with scarcely an interruption. The water runs down into the ear through the silks and rots the corn. In order to prevent this it is necessary to break every stalk just below the ear and bend the tops with the ears down so the water will run off. Later it is husked and carried to the crib, when it is subjected to the worst of all the evils, the black weevil. The eggs from which this insect springs are deposited in the corn while in the field and commence to hatch soon after it is harvested. I have personally tested this by taking an ear of corn from the field and after shelling it placed the corn in a bottle, which was corked up and set away. In about three weeks the weevils began to appear, and in six weeks every kernel was destroyed. At first I wondered why the Mexicans usually planted their corn in such small patches and so near the house, but in view of the foregoing facts this is easily explained. Almost the same vexatious conditions prevail in nearly everything that one attempts to do in this country, the variety and numbers of enemies and hindrances varying with each undertaking. There is a hoodoo lurking in every bush, and no matter which way the stranger turns he finds himself enmeshed in a veritable entanglement of impediments and aggravations.

All along and up and down the banks of the Tuxpam River, and in other more remote localities, there are countless wrecks and ruins of sugar mills, distilleries and other evidences of former American industry, which mark the last traces of blighted ambitions and ruined fortunes of investors. The weeds and bushes have overgrown the ruins and tenderly sheltered them from the sun's rays and the view of the uninquisitive passer-by. They have become the silent haunts of wild animals, scorpions and other reptiles. At the visitor's approach a flock of jaybirds will immediately set up a clamorous chattering and cawing in the surrounding trees, as if to reproach the trespasser who invades the lonely precincts of these isolated tomb-like abodes. They tell their own tale in more eloquent language than any writer could command. With each ruin there is a traditional and oftentimes pathetic story. In some cases the investor was fortunate enough to lose only his money, but in many instances the lives along with the fortunes of the more venturesome were sacrificed to some one or other of the various forms of pestilence which from time to time sweep over the country.

Among the native fruit products in this section the orange and the mango hold first rank, with bananas and plantains a close second. In close proximity to almost every native hut one will find a small patch of plantain and banana stalks. The plantain is made edible by roasting with the skin on, or by peeling and splitting it in halves and frying it in lard or butter.

Of all tropical fruits the mango is perhaps the most delicious. Its tree grows to enormous size and bears a prolific burden of fruit. In front of my house are a great number of huge mango trees which are said to have been planted more than two hundred years ago. The fruit picked up from under a single tree amounted to a trifle over one hundred and sixty-one bushels. Unlike the banana or even our American peaches, pears and plums, the mango is scarcely fit to eat unless allowed to ripen and drop off the tree. Much of the delicacy of its flavor is lost if plucked even a day before it is ready to fall. When picked green and shipped to the American markets it is but a sorry imitation of the fruit when allowed to ripen on the tree. It ripens in June, and it is almost worth one's while to make a flying trip to the tropics in that month just to sit beneath the mango tree and eat one's fill of this fruit four or five times a day.

The only native fruit that ever could be profitably raised here for the American market is the orange. The Mexican orange is well known for its thin, smooth skin and superior flavor and sweetness. The trees thrive in the locality of Tuxpam, and bear abundantly from year to year without the least cultivation or attention. On my place thousands of bushels of this fruit drop off the trees and go to waste every year, there being no market for it. I made an experimental shipment of 1,000 boxes to New York on one of the Ward Line Steamers. After selecting, wrapping and packing them with the greatest care, and prepaying the freight, in due time I received a bill from the New York commission house for $275 (gold) for various charges incidental to receiving and hauling them to the public dump. The steamer, however, had been delayed several days. The ratio of profit on this transaction is a fair example of the returns that one may reasonably expect from an investment in any agricultural enterprise in Mexico. If ever we get rapid steamer service between Tuxpam and Galveston or New Orleans, it is my belief that orange-growing could be made profitable in this country, but until then it would be useless to consider the orange-growing industry.

Having had some experience in farming in my boyhood, I thought I knew more about corn-raising than the natives did and that I would demonstrate a few things that would be useful to them; so I instructed my foreman to procure a cultivator and cornplanter from the United States. At Tuxpam I found an American plow which had been on hand perhaps for some years, and was regarded by the natives as a sort of curiosity. No merchant had had the rashness, however, to stock himself with a cultivator or cornplanter. The foreman was ordered to plow about fifteen acres of ground and plant it to corn as an experiment. The natives hearing of the undertaking came from a distance to see the operation. They thought it was wonderful, but didn't seem to regard it with much favor. The piece was planted in due season, and the rows both ways were run as straight as an arrow. It required the combined efforts of all the extra help obtainable in the neighborhood to rid the corn of the pests that beset it, but after cultivating it three times and "laying it by," the height and luxuriance of growth it attained were quite remarkable. Standing a trifle over six feet tall I could not reach half the ears with the tips of my fingers. The ground was rich, and as mellow as an ash-heap and appeared to rejoice at the advent of the plow and cultivator. One night in August there came a hard rain, accompanied by the usual hurricanes at this season, and next morning when I went out, imagine my astonishment to find that not a hill of corn in the whole field was standing! Its growth was so rank and the ground so mellow that the weight of one hill falling against another bore it down, and the whole field was laid as flat as though a roller had been run over it. It was all uprooted and the roots were exposed to the sun and air. We didn't harvest an ear of corn from the whole fifteen acres. The other corn in the neighborhood withstood the gale without any damage. This experience explained why it is that the natives always plant corn in hard ground, and also furnishes additional proof that it is usually safe to adhere pretty closely to the prevailing customs, and exercise caution in trying any innovations.

After clearing a piece of land for corn the natives will plant it for a couple of years, then abandon it to the weeds and brush for awhile. They then clear another piece, and in two or three years the abandoned piece is covered with a growth of brush sufficiently heavy so that when cut and burned the fire destroys such seeds as have found their way into the piece. After land here has been planted for a few years it becomes so foul with weeds that it would be impossible for a man with a hoe to keep them down on more than an acre. It is surprising how rapidly and thickly they grow. The story of the southern gentleman who said that in his country the pumpkin vines grew so fast that they wore the little pumpkins out dragging them over the ground would seem like a plausible truth when compared with what might be said of rapid growth in Mexican vegetation. They say that the custom of wearing machetes at all times is really a necessity, as when a man goes to the field in the morning there is no knowing but that it may rain and the weeds grow up and smother him before he can get back home. I am, however, a little skeptical on this point.

A serious difficulty which has to be reckoned with in Mexico is the utter disregard that many of the natives have for the property rights of others. Pigs, chickens, calves, and even grown cattle, are constantly disappearing as quietly and effectually as though the earth had opened in the night and swallowed them. One evening a native came in from a distance of twelve miles to purchase six cents' worth of mangos, and being otherwise unencumbered in returning home he took along a calf which he picked up as he passed the outer gate. At another time when the cane mill was started in the morning, it was discovered that a large wrench, weighing probably twenty pounds, was missing. There being no other mill of similar construction in the community, it was inconceivable that anyone could have had any use for the wrench. The foreman called the men all together and told them of the disappearance. He discharged the whole force of more than a hundred men, and said there would be no more work until the wrench was returned. Next morning it was found in its accustomed place at the mill, and every man was there ready to go to work.

Shortly after buying the ranch I was spending the night there, and went out to hunt deer by means of a jack,—a small lamp with a reflector, carried on top of the head, and fastened around the hatband. Assuming that the reader may not have had any experience in this lonesome sport, I would explain that on a dark night the light from the jack being cast into the eyes of an animal in the foreground produces a reflection in the distance resembling a coal of fire. If the wind is favorable, one can approach to within thirty to fifty yards of a deer, which will stand intently gazing at the light. The light blinds the eye of the animal so that the person beneath cannot be seen even at a distance of twenty feet. The hunter can determine how near he is to the game only by the distance that appears to separate the eyes. For instance, at 125 to 150 yards the eyes of a deer will shine in the darkness as one bright coal of fire, and as one approaches nearer they slowly separate until at fifty to sixty paces they appear to be three or four inches apart, depending upon the size of the animal. It is then time to fire. It is always best to proceed against the wind, if there is any, otherwise the deer will scent your presence. The eye of a calf or burro will shine much the same as that of a deer, and one must be cautious when hunting in a pasture. I took my shotgun with a few shells loaded with buckshot, and passing through the canefield came to a clearing about half a mile from the house. As I approached the opening I sighted a pair of eyes slowly moving towards me along the edge of a thicket next the clearing, apparently at a distance of about seventy-five yards. I knew it was not a deer, because that animal will always stand still as soon as it sights a lamp. It was too large for a cat, and did not follow the customary actions of a dog; but what it was I couldn't imagine. The two enormous eyes came nearer and nearer, moving to first one side and then the other, the animal appearing to be unaware of my presence. When it approached to within perhaps fifty yards of where I stood, I thought it was time to shoot, and so cocking both hammers of my gun I blazed away, intending to fire only one barrel and keep the other for an emergency. In my excitement I must have pulled both triggers, as both cartridges went off with a terrific bang. The recoil sent me sprawling on my back in the brush, the gun jumping completely out of my hands and landing several feet distant. The light was extinguished by the fall, and I lay there in utter blackness. When I fired, the animal lunged into the thicket with a crash, and in the confusion of my own affairs immediately following, I heard no more sounds. I discovered that I had thoughtlessly come away without a match, and being unfamiliar with the territory, had no idea in which direction the house stood. Groping around in the dark I finally located the gun and struck back into the brush in what I supposed to be the direction I came. Presently I ran into a dense jungle of terrible nettles, which the natives call *mala mujer* (bad woman). They are covered with needlelike thorns and their sting is extremely painful and annoying. I was also covered with wood-ticks, which added appreciably to my misery. It was cloudy and the night was as dark as death. Realizing that I was on the wrong route it seemed necessary to spend the night there, but I could neither sit nor stand with comfort amid the nettles. After proceeding five or six hundred yards through these miserable prickly objects (which in height ranged from two to thirty feet, thus pricking and stinging me from my face to my knees) I suddenly plunged headlong over a steep embankment into the water, when I became aware that I had reached the river; but whether I was above or below the house (which stands back about a thousand yards from the river) I couldn't tell. After groping my way along under the river bank for nearly half a mile, during the space of which I again fell in twice, I concluded that with my customary luck I was headed the wrong way, and so retraced my steps and proceeded along down the river for nearly a mile, when I came to a landing-place. Leaving the river I went in the opposite direction a short distance, and soon bumped into some sort of a habitation. After feeling my way more than half-way around the hut and locating an aperture (the door) I hallooed at the top of my voice four or five times, and receiving no response I ventured in only to find the place vacant. Returning to the open I manœuvred around until I found another hut, where I proceeded to howl until the natives woke up. I couldn't imagine how I was to make myself understood, as of course they could not understand a word of English. The man struck a match and seeing me standing in the door with a gun in my hand, and with my face all scratched and swollen to distortion from my explorations in the nettle patch, both he and his wife took fright and jumping through an opening on the opposite side of the room disappeared in the darkness, leaving me in sole possession of the place. After groping around the room in vain search of a match, and falling over about everything in the place, I returned to the open air. Meantime the clouds had begun to break away and I could see the dim outline of a large building a short distance beyond, which proved to be the sugar-mill. I was now able to get my bearings, and discovered that the hut from which the two people had fled was one of a number of a similar kind which belonged to the place and which were provided free for the workmen and their families that they might be kept conveniently at hand at all times. I was not long in finding the main road leading to the house, and when I arrived there everybody was asleep. After fumbling around all over the place in the dark I found a match and discovered that it was twenty-five minutes of three. Thus ended my first deer-hunt in Mexico. In the morning I noticed the *zopilotes* (vultures) hovering over the field in the direction I had taken the night before, and upon going to the spot I found an enormous full-grown jaguar lying dead about ten feet from the edge of the clearing. Several shot had penetrated his head and body, and luckily, one entering his neck had passed under the shoulder-blade and through the heart. The natives said it was the only jaguar that had been seen in that locality for years, and it was the only one I saw during the whole of my travels in Mexico.

That morning it was discovered that every hut in the settlement at the mill had been vacated during the night, and there was not a piece of furniture or a native anywhere in sight; the place looked as desolate as a country-graveyard. Later in the day we found the whole crowd encamped back in the woods, and were told that during the night an Evil Spirit in the form of a white man with his face and clothes all bespattered with blood, had visited the settlement, and wielding a huge machete, also covered with blood, had threatened to kill every man, woman and child in the place. A few years prior to that an American had been foully murdered at the mill by a native, who used a machete in the operation, and this, they said, was the second time in five years that the murdered man had returned in spirit-form to wreak vengeance on the natives. It was more than three months before they could all be induced to return to the houses. I cannot imagine what sort of an apparition it was that molested them the first time. The frightened native and his wife had doubtless returned and alarmed the others with a highly exaggerated story, and gathering up their few belongings they had fled for their lives. I told the foreman the circumstances, but he strongly advised me not to attempt to undeceive them, because they had a deepseated superstition about the mill, and no amount of explanation would convince them that the place was not haunted by the spirit of the murdered man, especially as this was their second alarm.

The peon class in Mexico are exceedingly superstitious and there is scarcely an act or circumstance but what portends some evil in the mind of one or another. About the only thing about which they have no superstitious misgivings is the act of carrying off something that does not belong to them.

Late one afternoon, while on a trip out through the country, we met an American in charge of two Mexican soldiers (in citizen's dress) who were returning with him to Tuxpam. They said he was a desperate character who had broken jail while awaiting trial for murder. He was seated astride a bare-backed horse and his legs were securely leashed to the body of the animal, while his feet were tied together underneath. His arms were tied tightly behind his back, and altogether his situation seemed about as secure and uncomfortable as it could be made. He was not allowed to talk to us, but the officers talked rather freely. They said he had recently killed an officer who pursued him after breaking jail. The poor fellow looked harmless and passive, and had a kind, though expressionless, face. His eyes and cheeks were deeply sunken and he showed unmistakable evidence of long suffering. They had captured him by a stratagem, having overtaken him on the road and pretending to be *amigos* (friends) they offered to trade horses with him. His steed being much fatigued he eagerly grasped the opportunity to procure a fresh one, and as soon as he dismounted he was seized and overpowered. The vacant and hopeless expression of the prisoner as he sat there bound hand and foot, and unable to converse with his own countrymen was indeed pathetic, and judging by his looks we were convinced that he was not a hardened criminal. We therefore determined to look him up on our return to town and ascertain the facts. Three days later upon returning to Tuxpam we learned that soon after we passed the party the officers had camped for the night, and tying their victim to a tree had taken turns at guard duty during the night. At about three o'clock in the morning the prisoner had managed to work himself free from the bonds and while the officer on watch was starting a fire to warm the breakfast for an early morning start the prisoner pounced upon him and seizing his revolver struck him a blow on the head which laid him out. At this juncture the other officer woke up just in time to receive a bullet in his breast which despatched him to the other world. Taking one of the horses the fugitive fled, and up to the time I left Mexico he had not sent his address to the police authorities; nor did any of them appear very anxious to pursue him further. The officer who was first attacked came to his senses a little later, but he was perhaps more interested in looking to his own comfort and safety than in attempting to follow the fugitive, with the prospect of sharing the fate of his fellow-officer. We were informed that the prisoner had been a poor, hard-working, and law-abiding resident who had migrated to this country from Texas several years before, bringing with him his wife and one child. He had brought about $1,000 American money, which had been sunk in a small farm near Tuxpam where he had cast his lot, hoping to make a fortune. One night his home was invaded by a couple of drunken natives who were determined to murder the whole family on account of some imaginary grievance. In defending his family and himself he killed one of them, and wounded the other, and next day was cast into prison, where he was kept for almost two years—until his escape—without an opportunity to have his case heard. Meanwhile both his wife and child died of smallpox without being permitted to see him, and were buried without his knowledge. It was reported that after his incarceration his wife and child had moved into a hovel in town, and that when the coffin containing his child's body was borne past the jail on the shoulders of a native, en route to its last resting-place, by a most singular and unhappy coincidence he happened to be peering out through a small hole in the stone wall, and saw the procession. He is said to have remarked to another prisoner that some poor little one had been freed from the sorrows of life.

How any white man can survive two years' imprisonment in a Mexican jail is beyond human comprehension; in fact we were informed that it is not intended that one should. I heard it remarked that "if a prisoner has plenty of money it is worth while hearing his case, but if he is poor, what profit is there in trying him?" The judges and lawyers are not likely to go probing around the jails merely for the sake of satisfying their craving for the proper dispensation of justice. We were told by one of the oldest resident Americans that if in the defense of one's own life it becomes necessary here to take the life of another, the safest thing to do is to collect such arms, ammunition and money as may be immediately at hand and make straight through the country for the nearest boundary line, never submitting to detention until the ammunition is exhausted and life is entirely extinct. The filthiness and misery within the walls of a Mexican jail exceed the powers of human tongue to describe, and tardy justice in seeking a man out in one of these Plutonic holes is generally scheduled to arrive a day too late.

With the exception of wood-ticks, the crop that thrives best of all in this part of Mexico, all the year round, is grass. There are two notable varieties; one is known as the South American Paral grass, and the other as Guinea grass. Both are exceedingly hardy and grow to great height. The Paral grass does not make seed in Mexico, but is generated from the green plant by taking small wisps of a dozen or more pieces, doubling them two or three times, after which they are pressed into holes made in the ground with a sharp stick, much after the manner of planting corn, and in rows about the same distance apart. Three or four inches of the wisp is allowed to protrude above the ground. It is generally planted thus in the latter part of May,—though at this season the ground is very dry,—because when the rains begin everybody is so busy planting and caring for the corn-crop that everything else is dropped. As soon as seasonable weather begins the grass sprouts and sends out shoots along the ground in every direction, much like a strawberry-vine. From each joint the roots extend into the ground, and a shoot springs up. By the early fall the ground is completely covered, and by the first of January it is ready to pasture lightly. The growth is so thick and rapid that it smothers the weeds and even many of the sprouts that spring up from the stubs and stumps. I saw a small patch of this grass that had been planted early in April when the ground was so dry that it was impossible to make openings more than two or three inches deep with the sharp-pointed sticks, as the holes would fill up with the dry loose earth. This patch was planted by a native who wished to test the hardiness of the grass, and with little expectation that it would survive the scorching sun of April, May and a part of June, until rain came. It was in May that I examined this patch, and pulling up several wisps I did not find a single spear that had sprouted or appeared to have a particle of life or moisture in it. But when the rainy season commenced every hill of it sprouted and grew luxuriantly. During the rainy season in the fall it will readily take root when chopped into short pieces and scattered broadcast on the ground.

The Guinea grass is almost as hardy as the Paral, but is planted only from the seed. It grows in great clusters, often to a height of six feet, and soon covers the ground. These two grasses seem to draw a great deal of moisture from the air, and stand the dry season almost as well as the brush and trees. The cattle fatten very quickly on them and never require any grain. Beef-cattle are always in good demand at high prices, and there is no other industry so profitable here as cattle-raising.

The deadly tarantula is as common here as crickets are in the United States, but to my astonishment the natives have no fear of them, and I never heard of anyone being bitten by one of these, perhaps the most venomous of all insects. They abound in the pastures and live in holes which they dig, two to four inches in the ground. One can always tell when the tarantula is at home, for the hole is then covered with a web, while if he is out there is no web over the hole. I have dug them out by hundreds, and one forenoon I dug out and killed seventy-two, often finding two huge monsters together. They sometimes bite the cattle when feeding, and the bite is usually fatal. Their deadly enemy is the wasp (*Pompilus formosus*) by which they are attacked and stung to death if they venture out into the open roadway or other bare ground.

The most deadly reptile is the four-nosed snake; it usually measures from four to six feet in length and from 2½ to four inches in diameter at the largest part, with sixteen great fangs, eight above and eight below. They have the ferocity of a bulldog and the venom of the Egyptian asp. The natives fear them next to the evil spirit. The most remarkable feat of human courage that I ever witnessed was a battle between an Indian workman and one of these snakes. In company with a number of other workmen the Indian was chopping brush on my place around a clearing that was being burned, and the snake sprang at him from a clump of bushes as he approached it. The Indian struck at the snake with his machete, at the same time jumping aside. The snake, narrowly missing his mark, landed four or five feet beyond. Immediately forming in a coil he lunged back at the Indian, catching his bare leg just below the knee, and fastening his fangs into the flesh like a dog. The Indian made a quick pass with his machete and severed the snake's body about four inches from the head, leaving the head still clinging to his leg. He stuck the point of the machete down through the snake's mouth, and twisting it around pried the jaws apart, when the head dropped to the ground. Four of the workmen and myself stood within fifty feet of the scene, all petrified with amazement. The Indian realizing that his doom was sealed stood for a moment in silent contemplation, then walked directly to where the fire was burning and picking up a burning stick he applied the red-hot embers on the end to the affected part, holding it tightly against his leg and turning it over and over until the flesh was seared to the bone. After completing the operation he fell in a dead faint. He was carried to the house and revived. His grit and courage saved his life, and in less than three weeks he was at work again. I offered a bounty of one dollar apiece for every snake of this variety killed on my ranch, and the natives would form hunting-parties and look for them on Sundays and rainy days. They were brought in in such numbers that I began to think the whole place was infested with them, when presently I discovered that they were killing and bringing them from all the surrounding country. They were so cunning that they would bring a snake and hide it somewhere on the place, then coming to the house they would announce that they were going snake-hunting, and in fifteen or twenty minutes would march in triumphantly dragging the snake, usually by a string of green bark.

There is in Mexico a small tree called *palo de leche* (milk tree) which produces a milk so poisonous that the evaporation will sometimes poison a person at a distance of several feet. The smallest infinitesimal part coming in contact with the mucous membrane of the eye will produce almost instant blindness, accompanied by the most excruciating pain. The only antidote known to the natives is to grind up peppers of the most powerful strength—as strong as those of which tabasco sauce is made—and pour the liquid into the affected eye. I saw this distressing operation performed twice while in Mexico. The natives naturally dread to encounter these trees when clearing.

There is an abundance of scorpions in Mexico. They are to be found under rocks and logs, and particularly throughout the house. One morning I found four snugly housed in one of my shoes. After putting my foot into the shoe the instinctive promptness with which I removed it from my foot reminded me of the army-ant episode when the boatmen so hastily removed their shirts. In putting on my shoes after that I learned to "shake well before using."

Among the nuisances in Mexico the fleas take their place in the first rank. They appear to thrive in every locality and under all conditions. Like vicious bulldogs, they are especially fond of strangers, and never lose an opportunity of showing their domestic hospitality. In connection with the flea family there is a very small black variety, the name of which in Spanish is pronounced nēwaw. They usually attack the feet, especially of the natives—for they wear no shoes—and burrow in under the skin around the toenails or at the bottom of the foot, and remaining there they deposit a great number of eggs which are surrounded by a thin tissue similar to that which covers a ball of spider eggs. The presence of this troublesome insect is not noticeable until the eggs begin to enlarge, when there is an irritating itching sensation followed by pain and swelling. The skin has to be punctured and the sack of eggs removed,—not a pleasant operation, especially when there are forty or fifty at one time. These insects thrive at all seasons, and, next to the omnipresent wood-tick, are one of the worst torments extant. I have frequently seen natives whose feet were so swollen and sore that they could scarcely walk. At recurrent seasons there is a fly that deposits a diminutive egg underneath the skin of human beings by means of a needlelike organ, and the larva of which produces an extremely disagreeable sensation, sometimes followed by fever.

This does not by any means exhaust the list of disagreeable insects and reptiles, but enough are mentioned to give the reader some idea of the bodily torments to which both the inhabitants and the visitor are constantly subjected.

Having obtained a fair idea of the existing conditions we may now return to our friend Mr. B., and then wend our journey homeward. After the visit to the hacienda of the wealthy Spanish gentleman (who, by the way, brought most of his wealth from Spain), he was perhaps the least concerned of any man in Mexico as to whether vanilla, rubber, coffee or anything else could be profitably grown there. Like Dickens with his Dora, he could see nothing but "Carmencita" everywhere, and no matter upon what line or topic the conversation turned it was sure to end in the thought of some new charm in the black-eyed beauty. She was not only a flower, but a whole garden of flowers, too beautiful and too delicate to subsist long in that vulgar soil. She longed for the life, excitement and companionship of the friends of her schooldays in America, compared with which the humdrum monotony of a Mexican hacienda seemed like exile. With ample means and social standing as an armor the conquest was therefore a predestined conclusion. The conquering knight returned home with me, but in less than seven weeks he was back again, though not by the way of the loitering route down the *laguna*. In the following November he returned again to America, bringing with him the coveted treasure whom he installed in a beautiful home in America's greatest metropolis. The union of these two kindred souls was a happy event. Their home has since been blessed with the advent of two lovely girls and one boy. It is therefore no longer true that no American fortune-hunter has ever returned from the rural districts of southeastern Mexico richer than when he went there; for here is an instance where one of the most priceless of all gems was captured and borne triumphantly away from a land which appears to abound in nothing but pestilence and torment.

Verily may it be said that this part of Mexico whose people, possibilities, peculiarities, pestilences and pests I have briefly sketched in the foregoing pages, was made for Mexicans, and so far as I am personally concerned, they are everlastingly welcome to it.

FOOTNOTES:

It was customary for the shipwrecked sailor to deposit in the temple of the divinity to whom he attributed his escape, a votive picture (*tabula*) of the occurrence, together with his clothes, the only things which had been saved.

The reader should not confound this with other Tuxpams and Tuxpans in Mexico. The name of this place is nearly always misspelled, Tuxpan, with the final *n*; it is so spelled even in the national post-office directory; but it is correctly spelled with the final *m*.

The mortality from smallpox in Mexico is alarming. Three weeks later our party stopped over night about twelve miles up from Tuxpam on the Tuxpam River opposite a large hacienda called San Miguel. We noticed when we arrived that there was a constant hammering just over the river in the settlement. It sounded as though a dozen carpenters were at work, and the pounding kept up all night. In the morning we inquired what was the occasion of this singular haste in building operations, and were told that the workmen were making boxes in which to bury the smallpox victims. It was reported that fifty-one had died the day before, and that the number of victims up to this time was upwards of three hundred, or nearly one-third of the population of the place. One of the natives told us that a very small percentage of the patients recover, which is easily understood when it is explained that the first form of treatment consists of a cold-water bath. This drives the fever in and usually kills the patient inside of forty-eight hours. There was no resident physician and the physicians in Tuxpam were too busy to leave town. They would not have come out anyway, as not one patient in fifty could afford to pay the price of a visit. A nearby settlement called Ojite, numbering sixty odd souls, was almost completely blotted out. There were not enough survivors to bury the dead.

I was told in Mexico that every day in the year is recorded as the birthday of some saint, and that every child is named after the saint of the same natal day. For instance, a male child born on June 24 would be named Juan, after Saint John, or San Juan. The anniversary days of perhaps thirty or forty of the more notable saints are given up to feasting and dissipation.

See description of the *tortilla* on p. 36.

After a lapse of twelve years I can recall the incidents and sensations of the journey from Tampico to Tuxpam as connectedly and vividly as though it had been but a week ago.

The customary measurement of money values in Mexico is three cents, or multiples of three, where the amount is less than one dollar. The fractional currency is silver-nickels, dimes, quarters, halves, and large copper pennies. Three cents is a *quartilla*, six cents a *medio*, and twelve cents a *real*. Although five-cent pieces and dimes are in common use, values are never reckoned by five, ten, fifteen or twenty cents. Fifteen being a multiple of three would be called *real y quartilla*, one real and a quartilla. In having a quarter changed one gets only twenty-four cents no matter whether in pennies, or silver and pennies. A fifty-cent piece is worth but forty-eight cents in change, and a dollar is worth only ninety-six cents in change, provided the fractional coins are all of denominations less than a quarter. If a Mexican, of the peon class, owes you twenty-one cents and he should undertake to pay it (which would be quite improbable) he would never give you two dimes and a penny, or four five-cent pieces and a penny; he would hand you two dimes and four pennies (two *reals*), and then wait for you to hand him back three cents change. If you were to say *veinte y uno centavos* (twenty-one cents) to him he wouldn't have the slightest idea what you meant; but he would understand *real y medio y quartilla*,—being exactly twenty-one cents.

In 1907, I received a letter from my foreman at the ranch, saying that yellow fever had spread throughout the Tuxpam valley district, and that upon its appearance in the American settlement at the *mesa* the whole colony of men, women and children literally stampeded and fled the country, taking with them only the clothes that were on them. The old gentleman (American) from whom I bought my place, and who had lived there for forty-seven years prior to that time, fell a victim to the yellow plague, together with his two grown sons. Thirty years before his wife and two children had fallen victims to smallpox. Thus perished the entire family. It is said that this is the first time in many years that yellow fever had visited that district. I scarcely ever heard of it while there, though Vera Cruz, a few miles further south, is a veritable hot-bed of yellow fever germs.

There is nearly an acre of coffee in full bearing on my place, but I have not taken the trouble even to have it picked. Occasionally the natives will pick a little of it either for home use or for sale, but they do not find it profitable, and so most of the fruit drops off and goes to waste.

A few years later Mr. A. sold his unimproved land for about one-third of what it cost him, so that now I am the only one of the party to retain any permanent encumbrances there. Be it said, however, to the credit of my injudicious investment, that there has never been a year when I have not received a small net return, over expenses; and that is far more than I can say for my farm in Massachusetts, with all its modern equipments. It has lately been discovered that that section of Mexico is rich in petroleum, and in 1908 I leased the oil-privileges alone for a sum nearly as large as I expected ever to realize for the whole place.

It will be understood, of course, that in speaking of Mexico I refer only to the district where I visited.

While this volume was in process of issue there appeared in several leading newspapers a full-page advertisement by some Mexican orange-grove company, which contained many of the most extraordinary offers. For example, the promoters agree, for a consideration of $250, to plant a grove of fifty orange trees and to care for them two years; then turn the grove over to the investor, who receives $250 the first year, $375 the second year, and so on until the tenth year, when the grove of fifty trees nets an income of $5,500 (gold) per annum, which will be continued for upwards of four hundred years. The company's lands are located "where the chill of frost never enters, where the climate excels that of California, where you are 500 miles nearer American markets than Los Angeles and 60 days earlier than Florida crops—this is the spot where you will own an orange grove that will net you $5,500 annually without toil, worry or expense. We will manage your grove, if you desire, care for the trees, pick, pack and ship your oranges to market, and all you will have to do is to bank the check we send to you." It would appear that anyone with $250 who refuses this offer must indeed be heedless of the coming vicissitudes of old age; for the promoters pledge their fortunes and their sacred honor that "when your grove is in full bearing strength you need worry no longer about your future income."